if the creek don't rise

TALES FROM THE SOUTH

First Edition
Printed and bound in USA

ISBN: 978-1-68313-071-0

Illustrations by Susan Raymond
Cover and interior design by Kelsey Rice

Dedication

Leo Augustus "Billy" Almand, 1923—1969

and

Robert Charles Hartney, 1919 – 2015

if the creek don't rise

TALES FROM THE SOUTH

NANCY HARTNEY

Pen-L Publishing
Fayetteville, Arkansas
Pen-L.com

Author's Note:

If the Creek Don't Rise: Tales from the South is a second collection of short fiction by Nancy Hartney. Southerners often intone 'the good Lord willing and the creek don't rise' as a supplication for help. The entreaty may have originally been a reference to the Creek Indians rising in rebellion, a threat along the early frontier until 1836. The 'creek' may also have referred to flooding streams and rivers that impeded travel. Even today, flooding creeks continue to be a problem in parts of the country.

The characters in these tales struggle to survive, find caring, and make a better life—good Lord willing and the creek don't rise

Contents

Postcard: Oaklawn Race Track, Hot Springs, Arkansas

Dear Sis,

Uncle Norton and me bet $2 each on the nose of a 50-to-1 long shot Saturday. Pretty exciting most of the race—our horse out front until the last turn when he crapped out and came in dead last. We consoled ourselves at the bar, got to feeling better, and then hit the betting windows again. By the end of the day, we were busted. Had fun. Guess that's worth something.

Luv, Angie

A Pound of Flesh

Usually the knot of backside workers did not cluster at the fence or place bets on the first race of the Oaklawn racing season. Mostly they were too savvy. Today was different.

Hands grimy from work, Darcy and Grace leaned into the fence, eyes focused on the red colt, Louisiana Tabasco. Elbow, with his usual penchant for being in the middle of any action, stood near the walkway and viewing circle.

From separate vantage points they watched the jockey carefully balance his weight above the withers, grab a handful of mane, and will himself one with the chestnut colt for the thousand-pound jolt out of the gate.

At the bell, the horse shot forward. He stretched low, legs digging piston-like into the track. Ears pinned, his red head thrust forward, the horse ran as if possessed, a freight train screaming around the oval. Foam flecks wet the bright silks. The colt charged down track and muscled through the field of horses into the far turn. Running wide, he settled into a long, wild stride, nose pointed toward the stretch. One length, then two, with the field a mass of flesh behind him. The colt streaked under the wire. Alone.

Grit and sand plastered the jockey. Fear and exuberance flashed across his face. He rose in the stirrups, fingers locked on the reins, and began a rhythmic pull-release, pull-release motion, praying for the track pony outrider to help slow the colt's mad rush.

Jim Hawkins waited until Tabasco, half way down the backside, eased up. He legged his lumbering draft pony-horse, Lady Spot, onto the track. They cantered alongside the horse a few strides before Jim attached the lead line, circled wide, and slowed to a trot.

Fractious, the chestnut flattened his ears and nipped at the stout mare, his teeth sliding over Lady's leather shoulder apron. Slinging his head back and forth, he kicked sideways and continued to mouth the bit. An oily sweat glistened along his neck.

"Damn horse crazy, too strong." The jockey spoke through clenched teeth.

"That's why they send me and Lady." Jim nodded knowingly. "She's the only horse steady enough to handle this rascal."

The trainer stood rigid at the track gate, his face contorted into anger. He fell into step beside the jockey and Tabasco. The horse continued to jig and snort in gunshots.

"Damn it all to hell." His face red, the trainer snarled at the jockey. "You've got to pace him. He's running like a bullet train. Throttle him down. Ration his speed, make him wait for you. You're the goddamn jockey."

"I tried. He's got his own mind." The jock jumped off, untacked, and moved toward the weigh-in clerk. "We won. That's what you wanted isn't it?"

"Not like that. He's got to listen. We move out of these mid-distance races, take on a long one, a route race, and he'll burn up before the wire."

Ears flat, the chestnut worried at the bit, saliva dripping, teeth clacking. He pawed the ground, tossing grit and dancing in tight circles as they moved toward the winner's circle.

The trainer stepped in close to the horse long enough for the track photographer to snap two obligatory pictures.

"Well, it doesn't matter to me. I don't intend to ride this horse again."

"You sorry sonofabitch. You think you can pick and choose what you do around here?" The trainer thumped the slender man on the chest with his forefinger. "You need every ride you can get. Don't think I'm begging you."

"I don't see no jocks lined up. You have trouble getting an exercise bug for this fool."

Ears back, Tabasco shook his head back and forth, rattling the bit. The crowd lingered, watched the unruly display until the small knot left the track, then chattering, moved on to the betting windows and bar.

Jim walked Lady down track, away from the throngs, for the next race. He felt her hocks falter several strides before they stopped at the rail. He frowned.

For the next two races, Jim and Lady drew green horses. The young animals did not run in the money and slowed immediately after the wire. He felt grateful for the lighter duty.

After the final race, with the track emptying, Lady shuffled toward shedrow. Jim nudged her out of the exit flow, dismounted, and loosened her girth. She snorted and lowered her head, following him. Dried, crusty sweat coated her chest and shoulders. Twice she caught a toe and stumbled.

Jim unsaddled the mare and slipped on a halter and woolen cooler. They began a slow amble around the row. He murmured to Lady. Her ears flickered back and forth, listening.

"My grand dame of the track. You've been a solid pony." Jim paused a moment to scratch around her ears and along her bridle path. "Your old joints can't take this treatment much longer."

With the crowds gone, three tractors rumbled onto the track, smoothing the surface for the next morning exercise rides. Dusk settled. Backside lights flickered on. Grooms moved businesslike between stalls. Workers sat in the aisles, talked trash, and cleaned tack. Horses snuffled around in fresh straw bedding. The easy groove of an R&B station wafted down row.

Jim slid the latch open, stepped into the stall, and poured Lady's evening ration into her trough.

His bay quarter horse, stalled next to the mare, thumped against the half door and nickered. A greedy animal, he plunged his nose into the sweet feed, stirring up the rich molasses odor. Jim laughed. The bay reminded him of an adolescent boy eating watermelon.

He did not hear Darcy sidle up until she draped her long arms across the half door, calloused hands dangling. "Use that bay. Give Lady time off."

Startled, Jim turned to her, then smiled. "Gelding's iffy. Race days with unruly horses and Lady is safer."

"Sunday's a short card. Don't think any of those rank hayburners entered."

"You're probably right. I have to replace Lady sooner or later."

"You and that horse been together longer than most marriages. Retire her. After all, you owe her something."

"Can't support two horses. Pastures don't come with apartments these days." Jim stood silent.

"Don't grab the dollar. Do the right thing by this mare. You know what the old timers say, squeeze the lemon, you get nothing but sour." Darcy turned away and melted into the evening.

• • •

Next morning, after workout, Elbow watched as the trainer and two grooms unsaddled the fractious colt. He leaned on his rake as they managed the colt's bath and started a cooling walk. Unable to tolerate the display any longer, he stepped around the muck bin and strode toward the knot.

"How 'bout I help you? Horse looks like he too much for y'all," said Elbow. He grinned. "Folks call me Elbow because I butt into conversations, you know, elbow my way in."

The grooms glanced at each other, then nodded.

"Darcy, girl, come here." Elbow hollered and motioned at a ruddy-complexioned woman who stood at the edge of the drama. She sauntered toward the men and leggy chestnut.

"Don't yell at me. You know this not my job. I finished my mucking. And my walking. I just stopped to watch you fools handle this big baby."

"Hoss be handling them." Elbow let loose with a guffaw. "Give him a song."

"You want me to help wrestle this hoss or sing him a church hymn? What's in it for me?"

"You know how hyped up he gets." Elbow turned to stare at her. "More he gets muscled around, the worse he acts. Besides, he likes the singing. Think of it like this here: we trade work for work. You sing and hand walk. I muck the stall and clean water buckets." He chuckled. "Nice distribution of talents."

"I only do this 'cause I like this horse. Not on account of you." She stroked the red-gold neck. "He's nothing but a macho baby. Sensitive. Person got to get on his good side first."

"Sensitive? That what you call all this acting up?" Elbow shook his head.

Darcy rubbed the colt's blaze. The animal lowered his head, ears scissoring, and nudged her chest, rocking her back on her heels.

"I been thinking on it. This here boy act good when you singing and handling him. He's okay when a woman rides him. Ever notice that?" Elbow cocked his head to the side.

"That and a wooden nickel proves what?" She hummed softly, slipped the bridle off, and adjusted the halter.

The horse settled. Stretching his neck, he planted his legs and delivered a full-body shake.

"You see, he relaxes when treated nice. This horse's got talent. We team up and tap into his good side." He handed her a lead line.

Singing in a rich soprano, Darcy led the colt down row, then stopped and turned. "That bug jock Grace can ride this big baby. We get a solid pony horse and between us three, we can get this horse straight." She struck up singing again and walked the chestnut toward the end of shedrow.

"Lookie here." Darcy grinned and sashayed past on the second loop. "He's a Sunday gentleman already joining the choir."

Elbow nodded. Humming, he raked the barn aisle, tines scratching rhythm to Darcy's melody.

The trainer stalked past, mumbling.

"Hey boss man, I got someone can handle that horse." Elbow paused and leaned on his rake.

"What the hell business is this of yours?" The man turned, face flushed.

"Got no business. Only trying to help."

"Just who do you think you are?" The trainer glared at Elbow, his eyes narrowed. "Who do you know that can handle my horse?"

"Darcy do it."

"The hotwalker?"

"That's the one." Elbow lifted his cap and scratched his balding dome. "Darcy and her friend Grace got special feelings for this baby."

"You mean that chapstick? The scrawny one?" Boss man grunted.

"Yeah. That one. Grace. She's working up her jock license. Horses don't care who ride." Elbow pulled a snuff tin from his hip pocket and stuck a pinch of Copenhagen in his bottom lip. "I know for a fact, them ladies love that chestnut hoss. Think he's special."

The trainer glared, silent.

"Maybe the best man for the job be a woman." Elbow cocked his head to one side and cackled.

The two men stood and watched while Darcy made another backside loop. The trainer shook his head and slouched down the row. Elbow watched Darcy and Tabasco a few minutes, then turned back to his work.

By the time he finished the fourth stall, he noticed the Livestock Sales and Disposal buyer talking to Jim Hawkins and glancing toward Lady Spot. Curious, Elbow eased in closer.

"That mare's stove up." The stock buyer nodded at the horse. "I'll take her off your hands now, before she goes downhill."

Jim stared at him and stroked Lady's neck. "You wear polished boots every day, never get them scuffed. You don't even touch the animals you send to slaughter."

The man hawked, leaned slightly at the waist, and spat. "You know well as I do, used-up ponies, spent racers and culls got to go someplace. Can't turn them out on the streets to starve. Besides, I can't get personally involved with every horse."

"Not happening today." Jim's lips, set in a thin, hard line, turned pale. "Maybe later."

"Whenever you're ready." Sliding a business card from his shirt pocket, he handed it to Jim. "Nothing wrong with a quick end. Humane. Kind. Think about it." He shoved his hands in his pockets and walked on down the aisle.

Elbow knew that meant one thing: the buyer offered Jim a deal. The mare, usable but old, couldn't work full days much longer. Jim, able to afford only two ponies in his outrider string, could not keep her. Devil take lifelong loyalty. No one said it. He just *knew*. That's when he hatched up his plan.

"What the hell you doing? Sleeping?" Darcy stood a few feet behind Elbow. He jumped and flared in irritation. "You know better than to sneak up on me. But, since you and Grace like that hot nuts so much, I can let you in on my plan."

"Plan? Who put you in charge?"

"Hear me out." He snatched the cap off his head. "You sing to that hoss. We get Grace to exercise that red fool and take the race ride. You use that spotted pony-mare to keep everyone steady." He grinned. "That colt learns to listen, relax, and act like a working race horse."

"Not going to happen."

"Why the hell not?"

"Jim's talking killer sell for Lady Spot."

"That deal not gone through, has it?" Elbow reared back and glared at her. He resented anyone that latched onto backside gossip before him.

"I expect by end of the season, she's gone." Darcy shook her head and sauntered toward the track kitchen.

•••

Over the next two weeks, Jim used the gelding for morning exercise. By ten, session completed, Jim untacked and led the bay to the washstand. The horse always snorted at the hose and playfully nibbled at the water stream. Crystal droplets splashed into the air, caught the light, and vanished.

Elbow stopped, buckets in hand, and watched.

"What's happening, my man," Jim turned the faucet off and led the gelding to the mechanical hot walker.

"How that bay doing? Shaping up to be a solid replacement?"

"Don't know, but I'm using him full time exercise days." Jim snapped the lead line onto the swing arm. "Lady's still handling race days."

Elbow scratched his chin. "I been consulting with my crew. They of a mind to offer you a deal."

"Crew? Didn't know you had a crew or offered deals."

"You understand we are a little short on funds." He stepped next to Jim with a conspiratorial wink. "But we offer you a way to keep Lady and save your conscience."

"Damn you. My horse and matters of my conscience are none—I repeat, none—of your business." Jim dried his hands on his pants leg. "Besides, the buyer's picking Lady up end of the season."

"Hold on, now. Don't be gettin' your britches in an uproar. Let's us not figure in no killers yet."

Jim squatted next to the gelding and began wrapping the slender black legs. Elbow bent down next to him.

"Me, Darcy, and Grace learning that red baby to mind his rider. He pay attention, that trainer take him up to a mile and an eighth. You know, take on the route races. Them ladies happy 'cause they love that fool."

Jim nodded. "He's got power but he's out of control."

"We got us a secret fix."

"Secret fix? What the hell?" He squinted sideways at the gnarled man.

"Music." Elbow leaned forward. "Between the music and no strong arm stuff, he settles right down. Listens."

Elbow handed Jim another wrap.

"And how's that work?" Jim paused and eyed Elbow.

"All in the training." He tapped his head. "Darcy pony that horse and sing. Grace rides. They trot the first exercise circuit together her singing. Darcy peels off at the sixteenth pole while Grace breezes the red boy on around. They come back, Darcy pick them up again singing. Every training day."

The men scooted around to the gelding's opposite side and continued wrapping.

"Where does my horse come in?"

"We got to have a solid pony. You know, a quiet one. Lady's it." Elbow's voice dropped to whisper. "Darcy be singing to that red nag any time your mare around—don't matter if they exercise, walking, washing, don't matter."

Jim stood and flipped the walker switch. The metal arms began a slow spiral and soft motorized hum. The bay stepped off with the motion. Across the yard, a hay truck grunted along the gravel lane, gears grinding. A barn cat sat and cleaned its face, fur glowing blue-black in the sunlight.

"Several problems with your plan. First, I've already called the buyer. Can't keep her and buy a replacement. I'm using her as my backup on race days. Second, this is none of your business. A horse is an investment, a tool. Nothing more."

"You wrong about that. She living, feeling animal. She worked steady for you over the years. Kept you safe."

"Non-working horse is a luxury, plain and simple. One I can't afford." Jim began washing the water bucket.

"That's where me and my crew come in." Elbow tapped him on the arm. "Listen, tell the killer deal's off. You let Darcy use Lady once a day with the red fool during exercise. My crew and me pay feed and vet bills on her. You keep ownership." Hands held wide, Elbow beamed. "We sort of lease her."

"I need folding green for another pony."

"That's the beauty of my plan. You use your gelding more, his training comes along faster. We pick up Lady's bills, you save, and put money aside. You have money when a suitable pony crop up."

"Nope. Can't see my way clear."

"Lady can handle morning exercise for one horse. Here's the sweet part—you run into trouble on race day with that gelding and need her, she's yours. She only needed for race days when the red fool running. You know that mare love to work." Elbow, arms spread wide, grinned and nodded.

Jim turned away. "Like the feller said, nothing wrong with a quick end. I've already made the call."

"Naw, man. You got to do *right* by Lady. You owe her."

"None of your concern." Jim strode off, his back rigid. He stopped at the tack stall, hand on the latch. "I'll be sure I use Lady as pony anytime that red colt's running. Consider it a favor to you." He barely glanced at Elbow.

• • •

Tabasco and the team fell into a rhythm. Darcy sang while she rubbed. She hummed to him over his grain. When he worked, she stood trackside, belting out every song she knew. Morning exercise, Grace jogged Tabasco light and playful, focused on control.

"Let me hear you say it, Mr. Trainer. I was right." Elbow puffed his chest out. "Them two saved your ass and make a nice horse out of that overgrown baby. I hear you have plans for putting him in a longer race."

"Let's see how he goes in Saturday's middle race."

"Right Mr. Trainer Boss. See how Saturday goes." Elbow tipped his cap.

• • •

Race day and the weak sun disappeared, leaving the track shrouded in sheet-metal grey. Of the starters in the sixth race, odds broke favoring Louisiana Tabasco with Grace in the irons as a bug rider. Spectators hung around the paddock, scrutinized the sleek animals, and made program notes. With the call "riders up," players disappeared inside, placed final bets, and crowded around the bar, eyes fixed on the race monitor. A few hardy souls clutched tickets and spilled onto the grandstand apron ready to watch the race in all its raw power.

Jim and Lady, assigned to Tabasco, were sweating by the time they escorted the jigging colt past the grandstand. He handed horse and rider off to the starting crew, noting a flicker of dread in their eyes.

Tabasco, usually unpredictable, pushed into the narrow gate confines and settled immediately, all business. Jim felt relieved. *Maybe those crazies could swing it.*

The field broke clean. Tabasco galloped easy, ears flicking, listening to Grace. She kept him mid-field, running smooth. As the horses fanned out on the home stretch, Tabasco clamped the bit between his teeth and bolted to the outside. Running wide and low, he zigzagged from outside to the rail and shoulder-bumped between two horses. Charging unchecked, he bumped another colt, throwing him off stride. Tabasco, running on his right lead, shot under the wire a length in front.

Jim legged Lady out onto the track, trotted through the sand, and attached a line to Tabasco.

The red colt nipped at Lady and plunged sideways, jerking Jim against the saddle horn. Arms burning from the strain, he struggled to steady the colt and keep him on Lady's offside. Twice he felt the colt kick. Lady grunted and strained against Tabasco, shoving him with her shoulder.

Grace relaxed her monkey crouch and hunkered back in the saddle, played with the horse's mouth in a vain attempt to distract him.

"I thought I had him. He simply stopped listening." She panted out her words.

"Needs more time. Maybe he'll get better." He heard Darcy hurrying along the rail singing "Oh What a Glorious Morning."

A sense of relief washed over Jim as he handed the colt off to the walking grooms. The tote board blinked: A challenge, leveled against Tabasco, cautioned players to hold their tickets. The colt had a reputation and, while the stewards were bound to make a judgment on the current race only, Jim thought the potential high for creeping prejudice.

After agonizing minutes, the board flashed the final order. Tabasco, disqualified, dropped out of the money. Grace had been unable to control him. At least, however, he proved he had stamina for the longer races.

• • •

The next day the buyer stopped at Jim's stalls. Morning workouts were underway and Jim had saddled the bay gelding. Lady stood against the webbing; ears pricked forward and watched the ebb and flow of people and animals.

Down row, the dull tap of a farrier's hammer signaled new shoes. Manure musk steamed up as grooms cleaned stalls. Occasionally a hoof thunked against a wood wall accompanied by a high squeal of irritation.

"I'll be back next week." The stock buyer did not push it. "You got my number."

Jim nodded. "Yeah, I got it." He paused and turned to the buyer. "How much per pound are they paying these days?"

Elbow, nearby, paused a moment to tug a bandana out of his pocket, wipe his face, and nonchalantly waltz to Jim's stalls.

Jim glanced up and immediately straightened. "I've made the deal on Lady. Buyer takes her last race of the season."

"My crew wants to sweeten the deal. Grace rides Tabasco in the Southwest Stakes." Elbow pulled his cap off, folded it in half, and stuffed it in his hip pocket. "We win this race, and she hand you the jockey's share of the purse for your next horse."

"*If* you win. That's a big if."

Elbow ignored the rebuttal. "You keep Lady's papers. We gonna add her stall fee to our deal. You already save up for another horse with what we doing. In the meantime, Darcy on Lady pony that colt once a day. Keeps everybody in shape and ratchets up training regime. Lady only gets used with that red boy."

"What happens if Grace can't control him? Or he folds?" Jim shook his head and turned away. "The Southwest is a mile."

"What difference that make to you? You take a chance with us and keep Lady. We lose, you still got the killers."

• • •

The day of the Southwest Stakes dawned sunny and cold. With Grace riding, the trainer, Elbow, and Darcy lined the rail. Jim and Lady led Tabasco to the gate.

With the final horse, the gate clicked closed. Horse-and-rider pairs focused on the track. An ethereal stillness hovered for a moment.

The high-pitched bell and "they're off" reverberated around the oval. Horses lunged out, a flesh-and-blood blur, and in six strides topped thirty miles an hour. The moment always amazed Jim. A lifetime of breeding, selection, and training unreeling in two minutes.

The announcer's voice gained in pitch as the race unwound. Fans crowded the rail, cheering. Bar chatter stilled as patrons turned to the race monitor. Box seat patrons rose, tossed dignity aside, and screamed.

Grace guided Tabasco to the outside and held him steady, slightly behind the pace. At the far turn, the field shifted as lead horses faltered and late runners made their moves.

At the grandstand turn, Grace positioned Tabasco mid-field, refusing him the outside swing, forcing him to focus on running businesslike and responsive.

As they moved into the stretch, challengers surged forward. The field, no longer bunched, strung out, fighting like drunks in a barroom brawl.

Grace touched Tabasco with her stick, asking for his reserves. He dug in, flattened into a blur, and lined up with a grey colt. The two ran head to head, barely a nose separating them. They flashed past the sixteenth pole and under the wire, straining within a half stride of each other. A handicapper's dream and a classic win by a nose. A grey nose.

Grace and Elbow led Tabasco back to shedrow. Darcy sang low and sweet. They took turns cooling the horse, pleased he had crossed the wire under control.

By Sunday, the ebb and flow of the track community slid to end of the season.

Elbow, heartsick, stood at the open door of Lady's stall and watched the tail lights of the stock hauler blink off as they pulled onto Highway 7, growling south, out of town.

"Damn it all to hell and back. Jim owes Lady a better deal." He shook his head.

Darcy ran across the yard, waving fanatically. Unable to stop the truck, she slumped, then coughed and stalked away, cheeks wet with tears.

• • •

That evening, Elbow made his way along shedrow for his nighttime check. Dusk carried a sleepy peacefulness with it. As the shed lights flickered on, moths intent on self-immolation fluttered against the screen-covered bulbs.

Tabasco stretched his long neck over the half door and woofed. He gleamed red-copper, even in the low light. Elbow stopped and admired the finely chiseled head, the pricked ears, and bright eyes. Arrogant and every inch a thoroughbred, the colt turned back to his feed.

Next stall over, a horse snatched hay from the net and shuffled around, rustling softly. The odor of alfalfa wafted out. Chance of rain hung on the air, dragging a wet chill with it.

Then, as if she always stalled next to Tabasco, Lady leaned over the half door and snorted, her coarse draft head juxtaposed against the refined profile of the colt.

They stood in contrast, a knight's charger and an elegant courser—mismatched, but perfect working companions.

Elbow laughed aloud, whirled and ran to tell Darcy.

A Ticket Out

She heard the horses before she saw them. They snorted in rhythmic breaths, bodies emerging in silhouettes through the grey dawn before looming whole, matching each other stride for stride. Sweat glistened on shoulders, ears lay flat, and noses thrust forward, straining for the finish pole.

Belle James clicked her stopwatch, freezing time in her hand.

That leggy chestnut filly with a crooked blaze. She go all the way. She done galloped off leaving them other horses with a face full of tail. Whoever named her My Ticket Out had me in mind. Me and Charles Allen aim at the big stakes races.

Belle ducked under the gate bar, her mind spinning as she waited for the exercise rider and horse to jog around. She slipped the watch into her pocket, snapped a lead line on the horse, and nodded. They walked off the track. Neither she nor the exercise boy spoke, careful not to jinx the red filly with their fragile dreams soaring too early.

"She's coming along. She'll be a good one." He popped off, gave the horse a quick pat and untacked. "I got another ride. You want me tomorrow?"

"Yeah. We'll breeze her to keep her loose, but not straining. She's got heart and speed. Just need to bring her along easy."

The rider slipped the bridle off and strode toward his next ride. Tick lowered her head for the halter, Belle buckled it, and they turned toward the barn washstand.

Belle moved her tongue into the gap between her two front teeth. Usually she felt shy about letting folks see that wide space, but today was different. Her mouth trembled on the edge of a smile and finally split her dark face into a show-it-all grin.

At the corner, the filly shied violently from a dark shape slumped against the wall, the whites of her eyes flashing as she reared. The lead line burned through Belle's hand. She scrambled to control the horse.

"Holy Jesus in a raincoat." She knelt and touched the form. "Charles Allen Davidson? That you? What in the hell happened?"

"They whipped my ass good. Beat me." His voice vibrated with a dark note of pain, breaths shallow and strained.

"Stay here. I be back soon's I get Tick settled."

Belle scrambled to her feet, jogged to the hot-walker, and fastened the horse to a swing arm. She slipped the saddle off, put a cooler on the filly, and set the walker in motion.

Returning to the barn, she knelt next to the man.

"You a mess for sure." She shook her head and sighed.

Eyes swollen shut, nose bent to one side, and blond hair matted with blood, the man attempted to straighten himself. A coughing spasm racked his body. He grimaced and rolled against the wooden wall.

"Damn them to hell." Hands balled, he cradled his stomach with his arms. "Them sumbitches broke my ribs."

"Gambling again. Am I right? Am I?" She shoved her face into his. "I done told you them mens are not to be played with. But no. You big dog, think you can handle them bookie cockroaches. Those people take it out of your hide. One dollar at a time." She grasped his shirt roughly, her hand claw-like. "Just need luck's what you said. Well, you got it. *Bad* luck."

She put her arm around his shoulders and helped him to his feet. They stumbled to a tack stall. He groaned. She half dropped and half eased him down on the straw. A water bucket hung on the wall. She placed it next to his side and began cleaning his bloody face.

"I'm hurting. Bad." He gazed up, eyes intense and pleading. "You help me?"

"You throwing everything away. Money, me, Tick—damn you straight to hell."

She wiped her face, worry lines spidered around her eyes. Her voice softened. "Yes, honey. I'll help. You my man."

Still moaning, he drifted into unconsciousness.

Charles Allen had been the first white man to believe in Belle's power to pick the right horse. He had told her she was magical. For that she loved him. His penchant for women and gambling, however, kept her off-balance and uncertain.

She put the word out her and him had a lover's tiff, that he'd gone squealing out and wrecked his car, injuring himself in the process.

"He my man, right or wrong. We partners." She thought her caretaking, for old time's sake, might bridge the chasm between her muck-worker status and his privileged owner-trainer world. He stayed in her ragged trailer, healing and grumbling about the smell of rancid cooking oil and cat pee.

Up every day before 4:00 a.m., Belle struggled to keep her grooming, rubbing, and mucking covered while she tended Charles Allen.

A week slipped past. Barely able to get around, he stood in the barn aisle and watched her brushing the copper horse. She ran her hand down Tick's crooked blaze.

"You my charm, my way to a better deal, my ticket out. You the best I ever had."

A striped barn cat jumped on the stall half door, sat perfectly balanced. The crossties jingled as the filly tossed her head and snorted.

"I need you to do something." Charles Allen shoved the cat off the door and draped his arms on the sill. He stared at her and twisted his horseshoe-shaped pinkie ring.

"Honey Man, you know I do anything for you. Tell me what you need."

"Enter Tick in the fourth race at Oaklawn next month."

She paused, one hand at her side, the other on the halter, her body rigid. "Arkansas? I thought we were headed to Illinois and a stakes race."

"Do what I tell you. A lot depends on it."

"That's a claiming race you talking about. Are you crazy? A trash race and someone lay down on her. Them mens knows which horses run good and they put in a claim ticket. No, sir, she don't go in no bottom feeder claiming race."

"You have to, Belle honey. I've worked a special deal with my creditors."

"Worked a deal? They not stupid. They take this filly. That what you want?" She turned away from him. "What kind of deal? This here filly my big chance."

"I know. I know. I'm scared, but I have to do this." He hung his head.

"You asking? Or you telling? You done traded this horse away in some crazy underhanded scheme, ain't you?" She ducked under the crossties and blocked his view of Tick. "We got no entry fee for no claimer."

"This'll cover it." He twisted the diamond ring. "I'll pawn it. You know I have serious obligations sitting on me. She gets claimed but I get a clean slate. It's all worked it out."

"You mean you got gambling debts. Which is exactly why you ended up stomped to a pulp. No. You find some other way. This filly mine." She turned back to Tick.

"Honey, honey. I bought this horse, she runs under my owner tag. Remember?"

"You *told* me she half mine." Belle stared at him. "*Remember?*"

"Well, yes, she is. But, do this for me. For *us*. They'll hurt me real bad if I don't get this thing straight. You hear?"

"That don't cut no string with me." She turned from him and brushed the horse with quick, hard strokes. "Besides, what makes you think I need you? I can go independent."

"Come on, baby. I love you. We can start over. We can do this thing together." He opened the stall door, stepped inside, and gathered her in his arms. "You know I love you."

"You asking too much. This horse an omen, a sign." She rested her head on his shoulder, one hand on the horse, the other at her side still holding the grooming brush, a sour taste in her mouth. "You love me now because you desperate. Minute you clear them gambling markers, you gone. I can feel it."

He put his hand under her chin and lifted her head. "You always stare right into the center of things. You've got a gift from another world for spotting horses and working them." He laid his sunburned cheek against her nappy hair.

"Sweetie, you know you my brown sugar. Right now, they got me by the balls."

His voice smooth, Charles Allen gathered her closer. "She's named My Ticket Out. You're right. She's a sign. Now she's our ticket out. Us two. Together. You have to believe in me like I believe in you."

"She's the best horse I ever had. It's my chance to move up to something better. You got no right to trade on my feelings. Don't ask me to do this."

"I know you've got a special thing for her." He stroked her arms and leaned on his heels, staring into her amber eyes. "You have a gift all right. You look at a nag, rub your witchy hands across it, and poof, you can make it into a winner."

"Always before I work for some other man. I got half this horse. You said you put my name on the papers."

"That's right. After the race. I'll put your name on the papers when we finish. You have to do this for me. For us." He kissed the top of her head, stepped out of the stall, and shut the door with the finality of a closing coffin. "I get the marker paid off and we can get Tick back."

"Where you going?"

"Pawn shop." The ring glinted as he twisted it. He shrugged and turned away, shoulders hunched forward as he quick-walked across the yard.

Off in the distance a dog barked, frantic and staccato. A potpourri of liniment, hay, and neatsfoot oil hung heavy in the cold air.

She buried her face in Tick's coarse red mane and stood shaking. Snuffling, she sank to her knees, brush still in hand, and sobbed.

Their musk-scent afternoons, lapping up salt tastes, meant nothing. His roving eye and insatiable gambling habit had knotted them together at the same time it strangled her. The horse had been his way of keeping her tied to him and her way of stretching for the I-want-it-all brass ring. Damn it but she still craved him.

Early January they shipped to Oaklawn.

A sick fear roiled in her gut with his mounting gambling debts. *He my man. I good enough to him and he be mine forever. Besides, Tick in the bargain now. He do me right.*

Belle's scalp prickled, listening as birds twittered awake, hailing race day with their choral rounds. Shedrow throbbed to life. Horses leaned over half doors, snorting gossamer breath clouds. Alfalfa and manure smells mingled. Jockeys drifted past and disappeared into the locker room. Railbirds materialized. Sports writers nosed about. Trainers and grooms conferred, solemn with heads together. Track officials scurried into offices.

She fed Tick and drank her third cup of black coffee. The striped cat sashayed around Belle's legs, purring.

By eleven o'clock Belle opened the half door and hung a webbed stall guard. She ducked underneath, knelt, and began to unwind the filly's leg wraps, whispering. The horse's ears scissored.

"You my dream. We show all them highfaluting folks what two Louisiana coonass strays can do. We from the swamps but you my ticket out. Charles Allen working for you and me. You'll see. Gotta believe."

Belle stroked the jagged blaze, her brown hand stark against the white hair. "Me and you like this here streak. We done travelled a crooked path."

Tick nuzzled the woman and woofed softly.

Belle continued her singsong murmurs and brushing right up to the time she led Tick to the saddling paddock and walked her around, showing off to onlookers. The crowd spoke in clipped tones. Day-trippers trickled onto the track apron.

Tick pricked her ears and snorted, mouthing her bit with a soft clinking sound.

Pungent smells of grilled hamburgers and sauerkraut wafted from food kiosks. Brunch cocktails loosened braggadocio tongues. Bettors groused over creased racing forms and rushed to track windows. Bodies moved in an adrenaline-laced waltz.

Belle led Tick into the ring for the house veterinarian. He checked the filly's lip tattoo against paperwork, nodded approval, and moved to the next horse.

"Riders up." The paddock master's voice rang clear.

Belle gave the jockey a leg up and patted his thigh for luck as the notes of 'parade to post' jumped into the air.

She led the chestnut horse through the walkway, passed the lead to a pony rider and watched as the jockey bridged his reins. Adjusting his seat, he jog-walked Tick past the grandstand crowd.

A tractor wrestled the starting gate into place. Pony riders cued horses up, handed off to start men, and stepped away as their charges moved into the narrow gate confines.

The jarring, clanging bell, lurch of horseflesh down track, and the ringing "They're off!" happened in heart stopping unison and morphed into a stabbing pain in Belle's head.

She spotted Charles Allen, his face in shadow. He bent to whisper in the ear of a leggy blonde and then guided her toward an owner's box.

She sucked in a ragged breath and let it out slow. Groaning deep in her throat all she heard was a rattling silence. Clutching the lead line, she still felt the live horse attached.

A claim had been filed. She *knew* it. Win, lose or draw, Tick was gone. She fought the urge to gag as she folded the lead line and draped it across a rail.

Let the man go. Let the horse go. Lay it down.

Eyes brimming, she turned blindly toward shedrow.

King David and the Bookstore

I sniffed the air. Unmistakable. Rank body odor hung in grey, almost-visible strings. Oh, damn. Only one person in the entire world smells that gamey. Sure enough, when I turned around, there stood David, in all his street-person glory.

I could see the Coca-Cola logo on a six-pack through his thin plastic bag along with what appeared to be a loaf of Wonder bread. Clothing, crammed into a second bag, spilled out past the handles. Another bag contained newspapers, lined notepads, scraps of paper, and a couple of books. Something sharp had started a small rip. He wore a brown shoe, mended with duct tape, and an odd black shoe—both without socks. A stained sweatshirt and a denim jacket tied around his waist completed his attire. Incongruous with his homeless persona, he appeared clean-shaven.

I drew back and breathed through my mouth, a reaction to the odor.

"David, what can I do for you today?" I put on my best small business-owner smile and began our ritual greeting.

"You can't do nothing for me, Missus Lola. I found one of your books on the bus. I brought it back." He pulled a slim volume out of his bag. A grimy hand with chipped and ragged fingernails gently pushed it toward me.

I sighed. In the Veteran's Administration Outpatient Clinic, David found an endless source of discarded and rejected books. He brought them into the store. Taking it, I murmured "Thank you." Small courtesies pleased him.

He had first appeared in my bookshop one red-golden October with his plastic bags. He wore nondescript glasses, the kind handed out by the free clinic. They were held together by a safety pin. He looked somewhere between down-and-out homeless and disheveled absentminded professor dignified.

"Did I ever tell you I was in the infantry? They sent me to Korea and it was so cold there I thought my fingers would freeze and break off. So cold you couldn't feel the heat unless you put your hands right in the fire. Cold enough you could see your breath turn to crystals in front of your eyes."

I sighed. "Yes, David, I think you did tell me."

Without stopping for a breath, he continued. "So cold I was afraid my ears might freeze and break off. Then I'd look strange. Suppose I couldn't even hear?"

I felt trapped. Although harmless, he was nonetheless smelly and unsavory in my tiny shop. Still, I thought him a puzzle and worked at balancing the contradiction.

"Did I tell you about my trip here?" he said.

His catch phrase signaled another story and I held my hand up, palm out. "I have to interrupt. Federal Express delivered six boxes of books this morning. I need to get them logged into the inventory and out on display. Excuse me." I called my part-time clerk to the front counter, gathered paperwork, USB drive, and fluttered away in embarrassment and exasperation.

"I know. I know. You have a bookstore to run. Remind me when you finish and I'll tell you about living on a ship." His words trailed behind me.

I stopped. "I thought you were in the Army. A ship means the Navy, doesn't it?" Too late, I bit my tongue. He had snookered me again.

"Both." He grinned and held up two fingers.

Shaking my head, I started toward my closet-sized office, glancing at him as he ambled toward the back corner and his favorite overstuffed chair. He opened his paper-filled bag, spread out, and settled down to write.

By afternoon, sunlight filtered through the window and transformed the nook. David, having dozed off, filled the entire cozy section with his pervasive snores and odor.

Customers wrinkled their noses, made comments about 'that man' in the back, and asked if I could check for a specific poetry book since they couldn't explore the corner shelves. I made a mental note to move the chair to the front bay alcove and trade it out for the hard church pew purchased in a garage sale. I didn't have the heart to make the swap until the shop closed. After all, I reasoned, harmless albeit smelly, he didn't come too often. Still, I found it hard to keep David's needs balanced against the shop's urban environment especially with the winter holidays coming.

The next week, undeterred, he followed his favorite chair to the front. The shop cat kept him company. He flopped his bags alongside, adjusted the window display, and spread his papers on the low table.

Old hippie customers and my regulars negotiated around him. Town clientele avoided eye contact and gave him an extra wide berth.

Each time he arrived, he stopped me with a story. I listened as long as possible, and then excused myself to help customers or restock displays. David never seemed to take offense until one day during a late Arkansas snowfall.

February had been especially bothersome, drab and frigid. Customers called and slogged in to pick up leftover books from previous orders, and tracked snow into the store which morphed into discolored melt. They complained about prices, groused over the weather, and then paid with credit cards, leaving moist coffee rings on the counter.

When the bell over the door tinkled late morning, I felt a rising irritation. *Oh, please, not another complaint.* I bent, wiped up a puddle left by the last customer, and stood.

"David." I groaned.

"Are you feeling okay?"

"Yes. Why?"

"You sounded like you have a stomach ache."

I stared at him. *Did I really do that out loud? Why me? Why today? Please, Book Muse, give me patience.*

"Did I ever tell you my mother named me after King David in the Bible? She said King David was a Jewish poet, supposed to be real wise and rich. She thought if she named me after him, I'd be like him."

I tried to smile but the stress of the morning weighed heavy. "Not today. It's busy and messy and besides, I'm facing hours of computer work."

"Well, did I ever tell you about the soup they serve at the church kitchen? Colored water. No pieces of meat and hardly any vegetables. Only chunks of potatoes. Did you ever hear of such food? How can a man manage on that? In this weather?"

"Now is not a good time for me." I rubbed my forehead. A headache threatened.

He stood before the desk, thin jacket zipped, newspaper insulation poking out, and blinked rheumy brown eyes.

I glanced outside. Snow was falling again and the wind had picked up. My heart sank. The cat sat next to the small gas heater beneath the bay window, her tail curled across her paws.

"You must find another place. At least today."

"The Shelter stays closed until 5:00. Bad weather, and people have to go someplace for the day." He stared at me. "They serve half-warm coffee and leftover donuts and preach at us. I don't need saving. I need a warm place to sleep. I need work."

How could I give a calico stray a place to live and not let a fellow human—even one named after a dead king that smelled like mildewed rags—spend a few hours inside?

I felt like a miser, no better than Scrooge. "Okay, David. If you'll sit in the back on that bench, you can stay until I close."

He glared at me for a long minute. "That bench is too hard."

"It's the best I can manage for today." I stood resolute while guilt flaked off me like dandruff. My headache burst into full bloom.

He continued to glare then turned and shuffled toward the back. His bags rustled accusingly as he moved through tables sagging with science books and navigated around a torrid romance display. *Oh, damn. My mother must positively roll over in her grave at my behavior.*

Throughout winter, David came into the store several times a week. He gave up stopping at the counter, instead staking out the hard bench where he spent the day writing or sleeping, feet mashed against the arms. At least, I told myself, he was warm.

April arrived daffodil yellow. Days dawned sparkling and warm, yielding to crisp nights until the year turned the corner into May. Customers brightened up with the weather, buying home project books and volumes of poetry. Holiday sales had been brisk and I felt the usual spring hopefulness. Neighbor passed neighbor, stopping to joke and trade news.

On the last day of the month, David came in, hair pulled back in a greasy ponytail. I had not seen him in several weeks. Weed thin, face sallow, and bottom tooth missing, he stood beside me as I arranged the vegetable gardening display.

"Did I tell you I'm going to south Florida? My daughter lives there and she wants me to come down. Wants me."

My mouth flopped open. I stared at him. "I never knew you had a daughter. Is this another of your tales?"

He gave me a wry smile. "Remember? King David liked the women. He had six wives. My mother never thought of that." Handing me a sack stuffed with notebooks, napkins with writing, and other paper scraps, he held my gaze a moment. "I know you like books so I brought you my poems."

"Poems? You write poetry?" I fumbled with the bag, held it a moment, and glanced inside. "Don't you want to keep these and continue writing?"

"I don't need them anymore." He shrugged. "Did I ever tell you about my third wife? She liked flowers." He pointed toward the front counter where he had placed a red Coke can with a single white jonquil.

• • •

Years have passed since I saw David. The calico cat disappeared. An orange tabby and a striped female replaced her. In the meantime, my little store continues to stock a few best sellers, regional books, and a stream of local authors.

A basket of paper scraps, each with a few lines of poetry or a haiku, graces the table near the cozy chair. Customers idly poke through the worn and smudged slips while waiting. Sometimes one captures the imagination and is read aloud—

a grasshopper on a vibrating blade of grass
dew on a spider's web
a cat dozing in the sun, predatory eyes closed
sweetness in the first bite of a fresh peach
a bird's clarion note for a mate

I smile and reply, "King David wrote that. They're a gift to the store."

The Girl Who Carved Wood

Spawned in the Atlantic, Hurricane Gustav chewed its way across the Gulf of Mexico, plowed along the Louisiana coast, and screamed into Terrebonne Parish September 2008. Kenetta's life changed irrevocably. Again.

She stroked the shrouded form then climbed out of the johnboat and tied it to the front piles with enough slack to ride up with the water, but not so much that it could spin loose. Her heart thumped wildly and her hands shook.

Mother Mary, Joseph, and Baby Jesus. Hard blow coming. Don't know I can do it alone. Damn your soul to hell, Papa. Damn you for your self-sacrificing ways.

Climbing the swayback steps onto the porch, she clung to the rough handrail and watched the boat rock its one still passenger. Tooter whined and sidled closer. Although the tri-colored hound offered no help, Kenetta touched him, glad to feel another living thing.

Mud and debris swirled around the chicken-leg stilt house, skinned onto the porch and slopped against her feet. She cursed the uninvited water that churned through the front, gushed off the back stoop, and rushed toward the

Atchafalaya River. Howling like some feral swamp creature, Hurricane Gustav swallowed living things whole.

Kenetta's stomach knotted in fear, bile rose in her throat. Rain, slanted and hard, slashed at her, rivulets streamed into her eyes and mouth.

"We'll be all right long as this old place doesn't fall over or the roof fly off." She and the dog faced the storm deliberately and stared into the coming destruction.

Kenetta Broussard, an olive complexioned girl-woman, had grown up on the edge of Chokeberry Bayou poling a pirogue through cordgrass and across open channels, first with her father, and later, only the hound.

Her father, Ramon Broussard, a barrel-chested rogue, drank bourbon whiskey straight, saying it had a tongue-softening bite and mellow undertone. His rakish blond appearance, despite a touch of grey and a protruding belly, drew women and made men cautious. Alone except for Kenetta and his dogs, he fished, worked odd jobs, and sold carved wood bowls, spoons, and figurines in French Quarter tourist shops. Sometimes he shipped hand-built furniture to northern galleries. He rubbed his soul into those burnished pieces of walnut, cypress, and butternut.

No one knew how he ended up in a rusted tin-roof camp house with a three-year-old child. Nor why he hunkered down on a god-forsaken bog, in a place with curtains so tattered that pieces floated out the window whenever a stout breeze kicked up. A broken mirror with flaking silver back hung over a board ledge. A sepia-colored photo of a toddler with a puppy slouched on the same shelf.

He lived with Kenetta and sheltered her growing years. Each morning he took her hand and walked the half mile to Sugar Cane Road crossing, where he put her on the yellow bus into St. Martin Parrish. Walking that road remained her strongest memory of his touch, her little girl fingers secure in his great calloused paw, his stride shortened to match hers.

As a girl, Kenetta squatted at his knee and watched him carve, her eyes steady on his thick-knuckled, gnarly hands. He twisted the wood under a chip-carving knife, working on bowls and figurines, while the yard curs sprawled in the shade. Stopping often, he showed her how to use the small palm knife to make willow reed whistles.

She grew older and he taught her to carve simple hounds, frogs, raccoons, and other figures. While they worked, in his soft patois, he explained the shallow-water pathways, great blue herons, bull gators, and water moccasins.

He talked.

She listened.

He carved.

She whittled.

He took whatever she made into town with his own carvings, returning later having sold this or that. He counted the bills into her pudgy hands. She grinned and crumpled the money into a Luzianne coffee can along with various rocks, feathers, and small bones that charmed her.

"Kenetta, honey, after a 'cane, you go out in that flat bottom and find you some broke-off limbs. You can whittle your little things out of those scraps." He nodded and continued carving, the piece changing in his hands. "Keep the cracks and insect holes you find in the wood. Hold on to those imperfections. They part of the wood's character, a record of how life happens."

"Yes, Papa." She watched him with the eyes of a curious cat. They carved under moss-draped oaks. Woodworking and swamp savvy became her treasured gifts from him.

"Papa, tell me about *ma mère*."

"She was an exotic Nubian queen. Special. Like you."

"Tell me more." She grinned and squirmed against the oak tree.

"Her hair grew in tight curls, knotted close to her head."

"Like my hair?"

"No. Your curls are soft and swirl around your face." He paused to stare at the sawgrass. "She had ebony eyes that stared straight into my heart."

"What color are my eyes?

"Your eyes are hazel." He stopped and looked off into the distance.

"Can I see into your heart?"

"No. If you're lucky, one day you'll see into some man's heart."

"Papa, why doesn't *ma mère* live with us?" She sensed his thoughts roamed in another place.

"She needs to live away. She takes care of someone."

"Doesn't she want to take care of me?"

"Yes, but she cannot."

"Who does she take care of?"

"I can't talk about that. Got to keep that creaky door shut."

"Why? Where is she?"

"You don't need to swim through that water again." His voice grew brittle.

"Yes, I do. I want to know." She stopped carving and searched his sun-webbed face. "If she was special, why those nuns come sliding by whispering when you take me to school? Why Mother Superior so stern? Sometimes Sister Bernadette cries when she talks to me. What's wrong?"

He did not answer. Her questions pricked and jabbed him.

The bellows-pumping croak of a bullfrog boomed across the water. A rival answered. Bell-clear, above the grasses, a swamp wren's sassy trill rose and hung in the air. Water striders skimmed along the river unfazed by the putrid, rotting vegetation.

With the back of her hand, she wiped sweat off her forehead and watched him. "What happened to *ma mère?*"

"That was a long time ago." He did not look up, but kept to his work. Laying his whittling knife down, he picked up fine-grain sandpaper square and made short, even strokes across the wood, willing the walnut to relinquish its hidden color. A humid breeze stirred the weeping moss strings, and afternoon light melted into evening.

"Memory's a funny thing." He carved, head bent over his work. "You got what happened and the place, but you get lost trying to connect what you *wished* happened and what *did* happen. Then you got to figure in what you want others to *believe* happened."

"I got a right to know."

"Be careful what you ask for. Truth's a moving target. Ain't always a good thing to know." He stood, brushed wood dust from his pants, and limped toward the house. A gaunt dog rose and followed. She stared after them, unasked questions curling in the air.

Downriver, a summer squall built up and dimpled across the bayou. A heron rose from fishing, great wings beating a fanfare toward the bearded cypress.

Often in the evenings, he sipped whiskey and sang while she played her reed whistle until the mosquitoes swarmed. She'd grow sleepy and he'd send her off to bed. Alone on the porch, he drank and listened to the night sounds.

Always, the next day, he rose early and walked her to the bus stop. Along the way, he urged her to learn everything her teachers offered.

"Papa, why do those other kids say mean things about me? They snicker and point and whisper."

"Sweet girl, they are small-minded people with muck at the bottom of their souls. They got no room for differences."

"Why those boys never talk to me in school? Why they hide and talk to me when no one's around?"

"Honey, those boys want you but they scared. Unsure."

"Scared of what?"

"Your beauty. Your color. Your smile. Your differences." He reached out and touched her hair, petting it into place.

"Why? Tell me straight, Papa."

"Lay it down, honey. Let it be." He fell silent.

One fine June day she graduated from high school. At the reception, he stood alone drinking strawberry punch, uneasy in the crowded church hall. Her face radiant, she laughed and talked with several girls until they drifted away in small clusters, already turning to new things. The good sisters hugged her and said she must remember she was special.

Kenetta and the old man left the school, walking slow, silent. They stopped near an eddy while he stared off across the bayou.

"Leave these gumbo ways. Go north." His face, lined with memories, crinkled. "Quit this swamp before its hypocrisy smothers you."

She stared at him, head cocked to the side.

"Don't give up the carving." He touched her face. "Wood got life you can hold onto. It's only thing I can ever give you. "

"I know Papa. I'll keep it. But all I really want is your love." She held his work-hardened hand and they turned toward home.

He built an architect's table that tilted and locked into a standing desk. She crafted inlaid boxes, carefully preserving the imperfections in the grain. He constructed slat-seat maple funeral chairs that folded flat. She worked on burl-wood bookends.

A year, then two spun out before she stuffed her woodworking money in her pocket and gathered the coffee can. "Papa, I'm woman grown. I need to find *ma mère*."

"You can't find her." He glared at her, his eyes narrowing.

"You know where she is, don't you? You can help me."

"No."

"I need to find out about her and why we live out here and why she doesn't take care of me."

"Go north for a few years. Learn different ways. We can talk after you see a different world. Different people."

She drove north in a faded blue '61 Chevrolet, windows open. The spotted hound sat on his haunches in the passenger seat, tongue lolling out, long ears flapping.

• • •

In Chicago, she wandered down the mile-long Gold Coast, swimming in the harsh city racket. An oily stink of stalled traffic clogged her nostrils and heat shimmered in watery waves across parking lots.

After a month, she rented a room in a dilapidated row house and connected with a wood vendor. Several blocks down, she found a Creole restaurant that advertised authentic Louisiana bayou dishes. Glancing at the posted menu, she sashayed in the door and could practically hear the owner salivate.

He whistled low. "What are the odds a fawn-colored girl with a Cajun accent would come waltzing in?" He hired her on the spot, a hostess in his faux Acadian world.

At night after work, in her rented room, she carved. She forgot the sharp clang of pots and dishes, acid insults from the chef, food gone cold, and customers' slights as she felt the wood morph in her hands. *Strange to move to the big city for a new beginning, yet work in a Creole restaurant and carve. A frayed thread to Papa and his festering secrets.*

Kenetta met Langston Davis her third day at work. Shirtsleeves rolled above a snake-entwined, black rose tattoo, he showed off his drink-mixing skills and joked with the customers. Fascinated with his blond ponytail and feline grace, she watched him. Often, she felt his brown eyes following her as she guided customers to white-cloth tables.

"Kenetta, I know a man who owns a place near Michigan Avenue." Langston leaned on the bar. "I can talk to him about taking on your work."

She arched an eyebrow. "How did you know I carved?"

"Saw you one Sunday in Grant Park."

"I go to watch the gulls and listen to their squawking, to carve outside. It reminds me of home." She paused and considered him, gauging his sincerity.

"Man I know owns the Rock Island Line Gallery. He says folk art's the rage. The trend keeps building but he wants something unique, yet elegant. You know, something upmarket."

She pressed her lips into a thin line and stared down at her short nails and blunt fingers. "Most folks think of Appalachian paintings and doll work, not carvings from Louisiana swamps."

"I'll introduce you if you'd like." He paused, sat a sweating beer before a mid-afternoon customer, and returned to the conversation. "His gallery's not too far from the Old Water Tower, a little north of the Wrigley Building. You know, in that high-end district."

She nodded. A sense of excitement and dread washed over her.

They arranged a visit.

An introductory launch of her pieces and her life changed, again.

Cool, fashionable people bought her work without any awareness of her heart's fragments massaged into the wood. They chattered about folk style and primitive art and rough sophistication. She felt her soul flutter away as they drank champagne and paid with credit cards.

Sunday afternoons changed also. Kenetta and Langston fell into a lovers' rhythm. With sunlight pouring in the window, bodies sweat-slick, and sheets kicked off on the floor, they took an hour licking and fingering each other before they got down to serious lovemaking. Other nights, spiced with weed and whiskey and blue musk odors, she'd float off into another world. Alone.

Such times, she heard the old man's bass voice, quiet-like.

"Your mama was the only woman I ever loved."

Her expression would change from puzzled to cloudy.

"Even over me?"

"Yes, even over you. I got loving feelings for you too, but my heart's tired."

Such times, he'd lapse into humming of lost love and heartache.

• • •

Kenetta recognized the tinny voice of the Methodist preacher woman as soon as she picked up the phone and said hello.

"Your Papa done stroked. Heart trouble I think. No one can be sure." The preacher spoke bluntly. "You need to get on home take care of this. You hear me?"

"What happened? What are you talking about?"

"Federal marshal come through here looking for him. Seems they think he killed a woman down in Houston sometime back."

"Did they arrest him?" Dread washed over Kenetta.

"No. Old Man got his sources too. He found out the law asking about him and took off for deep swamp. He's hiding out with some of your mama's people. Them badges still sniffing around."

"How bad is he?"

"He's not going to last."

She left Langston and the gallery and the restaurant, aimed the rusted Chevy beater from Chicago down through St. Louis and Memphis to Louisiana. Her heart thumped in her throat the entire night and all the next day as she drove, her life becoming more uprooted with every turn of the wheels.

Old Man, still alive when she arrived late Thursday, smiled and petted her face. She bundled him up and spirited him to their clapboard stilt house. Under the water oak, their roles reversed.

She carved.

He watched.

She talked.

He listened.

She stared into the present.

He murmured about the past, yearned for the other side and hummed wordless songs.

When he nodded off, she paddled into the moss-bearded dimness with Tooter. There, musk turtles slid from dead stumps into black water and ibis moved without a trace through green scum. Returning in late afternoon with a cache of collected wood and a mess of frogs or bass, she cooked. He'd rouse up and pick through his plate while she ate with gusto and licked her fingers.

"Hurricane season coming." He shifted in his chair. "I ain't riding through another one. Got no will left."

"You ready to quit and die?"

He grunted and stared off with rheumy eyes.

"If you're dying anyway, Papa, tell me about *ma mère*."

He slumped, drool sliding out of his mouth, eyes fixed on something unseen. A breeze carried the scent of decay, things long rotted and those recently dead.

"You go in the house. Get that picture of you and that dog off that board shelf. Bring it here." His words staggered out, misshapen and bent.

She nodded and returned with the small framed picture, sat while he popped the back off, and fumbled out a hidden sepia-tone snapshot.

"This here your mama." His hand shook as he laid the picture on her lap.

Kenetta stared down at a chocolate-faced woman holding a creamy baby in one arm with the other hand draped around a dark, lanky boy. Neither smiled. The baby squinted in the sun.

"You see, honey, we met up in the Bywater near the Florida Projects over to New Orleans. She had a boy when I met her. He always in trouble. He given over to rages and tantrums. Older he got, worse he got. She thought we'd best go live with some of her people in Houston. See if he could get straight in another place."

He paused and wiped spittle from his chin. "We loved him and tried to do right, but weren't no use. He turned seventeen and knifed up a man bad in some fight over craps. Since they was both black and nobody got killed, judge give him the choice between Army enlisting and jail. Not his first time for law trouble."

"He's my brother?"

"Half-brother. We waited twelve years to have you cause she afraid of having another bad one. Kept saying it was her fault he turned bad."

"But what happened to them?"

"Boy wouldn't pay no mind to anyone. She kept after me to take you and go live some other place while she raised up the boy. Ever' time he got into trouble, she'd tell me leave. That last time, she begged me—*begged on her knees*—to take you and go live away, raise you up white. My heart cracked open. You turned three. I packed up and left like she wanted."

"Why? Lots of men around here got black women and mixed children. Lots of people got sheriff trouble."

"It's not the white fornicating with black and spawning babies. Not the law trouble. Not even the marrying before some country preacher. It's *hiding the race* of the children, helping them *cross*. Scares white people real bad to think about Negro blood seeping into their family unknown."

Kenetta held his bony hand, traced thin scars with her fingertips.

"That boy come back from Nam messed up bad. Drugs. Killing. Crazy." Tears streamed down Old Man's face. He made a sound between a sob and a croak. "He splattered meanness over anyone around him. He sneaked off from the Army early and crawled back down to Houston. Went straight to her. Kept after her to tell where we was. He know'd her and me stayed in touch.

"One day, he got to beating her with a carving I'd made for her. It were a pregnant goddess. He kept beating, trying to find where you and me living. She didn't tell him, but he figured it weren't in Texas. He finally killed her. He run and tried to pin it on me."

The dog whined and edged close, leaning into the man. With the back of his hand, he wiped his nose, smearing mucus in a glistening line.

"Talk that finally got passed to me was that he living AWOL, hiding out, and needing money for his meanness." He stared off toward the river. "Sumbitch thought he could get what he wanted if he found us. He snuck up to New Orleans and hid in the Ward. He'd steal. Crank up. Knife anyone got in his way." Old Man squeezed his eyes shut and tilted his head back.

"When money ran low, he'd start in asking 'bout us again. He never give up, figuring he could jack me for whatever he needed."

Steadying himself, he stared at her. "But I got friends too. They sent me word about what that boy doing. They understood what was needed.

"After you drove off, I couldn't let it go no longer. That boy too close." He stared down at his hands. "I had to get on with business."

Old Man straightened his drooping body and struggled to control his trembling. "I slip off to the Ward and find him where he put that glass gun in his arm." He rocked and cried, holding himself as if fearful pieces would fly asunder.

"Never a word passed between us. Soon's he see me, he understood. Didn't fight. He too messed up on them drugs.

"I cut sumbitch's throat. Knife had a fine edge. He never felt a thing. I held him 'til the spurtin' stopped. I sat there on the linoleum rocking. Held him 'til dark come and his blood jelled up."

He stared off into nothing. "My people passed word on down that the law sure enough dogging after me."

The wind ceased. Wild creatures fell silent. Visible clouds of flying, biting mosquitoes swarmed over the water. He bent forward and watched steel-colored clouds roil along the river.

"Both our souls going to hell. Him and me. We each dragging the other straight to Old Scratch." He grunted, swayed back and forth, and hugged himself.

"I never see my love again." Muscles in his throat twitched and his Adam's apple bobbed.

"I'm here, Papa. Stay with me. Love *me*." She sat in front of him, hands lightly touching his knees. Her mouth grew dry and her thoughts raced.

"She loved you. I care for you 'cause she's in you." He shook his head slow-like and smiled, stroked her cheek with a gnarled, chapped hand. "Too late. The Black Prince already kissed me. He holding me next to his dark heart."

"Papa, look at me." She held his face in her hands and studied the wrinkles. "Hold *me* near your heart. Live for *me*."

"I'm not gonna stay in this here swamp for another 'cane blow." He sucked in a deep breath and let it out ragged.

"My time is done. I need to lay down. You'll be okay without me."

He died midday when Hurricane Gustav touched landfall along the southwestern coast. She rolled him in a sheet and put him in the pirogue under a tarp, snugging it tight. Her hands shook as she tethered the boat with clumsy knots.

Finished, she climbed the swayback steps and stood on the porch with Tooter, face turned into the coming fury.

"Mother Mary, Joseph, and Baby Jesus. A hard blow coming. Don't know I can do it alone. Damn you for dying Papa. Damn you for your self-sacrificing ways. Most of all, damn you for not telling me."

She howled agony into the wind until her throat grew raw and her voice gave out. Holding onto the porch rail, she sobbed, chest heaving. Tears streamed down her face and mixed with rain.

The storm hacked across the swamp, ripped apart trees and lacerated lives, washed the marsh clean.

A mud-caked calm descended as Gustav spit out its last wet torment and shifted east. Quiet settled on the bayou. Alone, she watched night descend.

At sun-up, she untied the johnboat, patted the wrapped form, and poled down the river to Greenford Canal. The dog stood in the bow, ears flapping in the wind. A passing fisherman gave them a lift to the parish church.

A crone played the piano. The preacher woman sat silent next to Kenetta, both lost in thought. As soon as the last note faded, the crone slammed the cover over the keys.

"Y'all finish up. I gots to get home before God gets me mixed up in this here mess and puts your sins in my lap. Besides, with all this water, I'm likely to drown or get mired up if I wait any longer."

"You go on, *grandmère*." Kenetta smiled and nodded. "I thank you for playing. Papa loved music." She sat on the hard pew and listened to the departing footsteps reverberate against the wood flooring.

No white man's going to take me, thinking I'll taint his family. Black man's going to pull me into a world I don't understand, expecting me to follow his people. Sins of others staining my living.

Her thoughts wandered the Chicago streets. Her body craved Langston. She smelled motor oil and asphalt heat, felt the wind off Lake Michigan, and heard the gulls cry. She missed the gallery, missed the restaurant.

Closing her eyes, she drifted through the swamp waterways. The odors of bayou decay, scream of a she-panther, and croaking of frogs curled around her being. Nights filled with a chorus of unseen life enveloped everything.

Two worlds. The same. Different.

She opened her eyes, stood, stepped to the coffin, and looked down on his waxy face. Her heart convulsed through a fog of grief. Gently, she tucked a bottle of Wild Turkey and a willow-reed whistle into the coffin.

The preacher woman got up and put an arm around Kenetta. They stood, heads touching, silent.

"Think about this. Every time a 'cane comes through, it washes our swamps clean and puts a layer of mud over dead stuff. New things sprout up out of the old." Preacher hugged Kenetta, kissed her on each cheek, and strode out of the dilapidated sanctuary.

Kenetta closed the coffin lid and turned back toward the world.

In the bayou, under the shade of the moss-shrouded water oak, Kenetta felt a gauzy affection brush her face and gently settle on her shoulders. Sunlight played across the water. Contented, she carved until the gators started bellowing and the mosquito clouds swarmed. Such times, the frogs croaked hoarse and plopped into the water, leaving widening circles that disappeared into the river's flow. Sulfur smells bubbled up. Alone, she stayed outside until the light faded from orange to ink dark.

"Time to go inside. Swamp spirits rising up, growing restless, gathering to tend to their business. We best leave them to their haunting."

She patted Tooter's head and closed her eyes, feeling peaceful. Life throbbed sweet around her.

The Bull and the Kitten

Udean had found the scrawny kitten with pus-matted eyes just as she finished the milking and turned the cow out into the south pasture.

She poured a pie tin of warm milk for the barn cats and watched when they crowded around, a greedy pinwheel of colors. Sick, the kitten lacked the strength to push forward even to eat.

Amos stomped into the passageway. "Don't fool with that thing." He growled, the craggy sound spilling through his discolored teeth and chapped lips. "I'll knock the miserable creature in the head later today."

"No, Amos. I'll keep it. Let it be." She stooped and lifted the ball of grey fur. Mouth open in soundless supplication, the kitten hung listless in her hand.

"The mama cat's dead. I'll feed this one and see what happens."

"There's no time for sick things. Barn cats live on their own."

"It's a baby, too small to survive alone." Udean turned and glared at him, the wet-rag kitten dangling.

"We don't need another useless thing to feed." He grumbled, then hawked and spat onto the barn floor.

He turned and tossed a full hay bale into the bull's lot. The animal snorted and butted its head against the barn panel, tossing strings of mucus across the ground, his neck and shoulders a solid mass of muscle. Fat testicles, jewels in a delicate skin sack, swung between his legs.

"He needs to stay out of the north pasture today," Amos jerked his thumb toward the lot. "That fool Polack has his cows next field over. I don't want the bull fighting through the fence to get at them."

"That animal is dangerous. We got no need for him now with only a few cows left."

"I ain't paying no potato head for the use of a bull pecker every time them cows need a squirt."

"Cheaper to pay for the humping than support that brute." She gestured at the bull before sloshing toward the house with the milk pail and the kitten.

She knew Amos detested weakness and that he took special pride in the Guernsey bull, a personification of his manhood and power over the farm creatures.

"Hear me, you hussy. Mind the bull." He hollered behind her. "And get rid of that useless rag."

Ignoring his shouting, she clumped up the swayback steps and strode into the house. The screen door slapped behind her.

Carefully, she placed the bucket on the counter, turned on the single light bulb above the kitchen sink, and sat the kitten on the floor.

She strained the fresh milk into a stoneware crock, put it in the refrigerator, and then squatted and picked up the kitten.

"I'll feed you and clean up those pus-eyes, but you'll have to decide to live. Can't lose your will." She dipped her finger in a cup of milk and, drop by drop, fed the weak grey form.

Her big-boned frame often made Udean feel like a work-horse, a heavy draft animal. Married to Amos for thirty-two years, she realized he no longer viewed her as a wife but simply a farm worker, a childless husk of a woman.

Year in and year out, she rose before daybreak, brewed coffee, prepared a thin breakfast, and trailed Amos to tend stock and begin their labors. One day fit into the following day, and the next, until the years nestled in an unchanging lump. *Where did they go?* She stared out the kitchen window, watching the orange-and-white cow amble further into the pasture, grazing as she moved.

And what of my love for Amos? Was it there when he courted me or was I just thrilled with his attention?

• • •

She had wed before a Georgia justice of the peace, heedlessly ignoring her stepfather's warnings. Slender, young and given over to laughter, she accompanied Amos to his farm on the edge of the Piedmont Plateau before it rose into the Blue Ridge Mountains.

A town girl, she had delighted in the nanny goats and frolicking kids. She breathed the acid hog musk, tasting it on the air. She felt comfort in the solid, placid nature of the milch cow. She watched wild creatures shyly tiptoe into the farm periphery and delicately steal from the garden. Amos groused at their thievery while she murmured "bon appétit."

After the fifth miscarriage, he stopped coming to her bed and turned to the drink. She felt her body grow thick as her auburn hair grayed and thinned. Had it not been for the animals, the drab loneliness that encroached would have been unbearable.

The small farm yielded little while the neighboring farms, with better land, thrived. Amos worked hard, making a modest living from the peanut crops, a few cows, and hogs. Red hens provided eggs enough to supply their needs, with surplus sold for extra pocket money. Her hands, once slender and delicate, grew rough and cracked. Her knuckles protruded.

Early one year, a farmers' cooperative opened under a federal grant in the county seat. Neighbors urged her to join. She began making cheese, at first simply as added income for her household expenses, and later as a salve to her loneliness.

Udean never missed a market during summer season. She talked with other vendors, enjoyed the company of women, mingled with neighbors, and listened to community news. She relished the chatter and rural bustle. Red peppers, kale, and purple turnips tickled her senses. Zinnia and daisy bouquets delighted her. The farmers traded among themselves and briskly sold to town shoppers. Her brown eggs and cheeses went early, but she lingered until the market closed in mid-afternoon despite her sold out table. Each week she bought a copy of the *Union County Herald Record*, a community newspaper, read it page by page, and carried it home to reread.

"Why not take the *Record* by mail?" said the skinny tomato vendor. "That way you can get the news even when the market closes down for the winter."

"Oh, Amos would never allow that."

"Your cheese money can pay for it. He's got no say. Besides, this is a time of women's liberation. Gloria Steinem said to pull off your bra and whip him about the head if he criticizes." The vendor hooted and clasped Udean across the shoulders. At that, both women laughed until tears ran.

Gradually, Udean experimented with adding home-grown herbs to her cheeses. Local town women and the grocer bought her weekly special. She milked a second cow and, later, a nanny, adding goat cheese to her stock. Young urban couples drove out from Atlanta, stopped by the market, discovered her cheeses, and immediately labeled them country gourmet. She basked in the compliments and attention. And charged double.

• • •

Four times during that first day, she paused to feed the kitten. In between, it slept. She rose twice during the night to care for the little thing. By the next morning, she found it sitting near its bowl in the kitchen, meowing.

"Get rid of that thing," Amos demanded. He sat, elbows propped on the table. "You got other work that needs doing."

"No, Amos, it's no trouble." She glared straight into his eyes. "How can I bear this place without something that *needs* me?"

He glowered at her, then stared down into his black coffee.

"The stock needs tending."

"Stock? You mean those cows and hogs? Even the goats?" She snorted and shook her head. "We sell those things. We *live* off their flesh and blood." She partially leaned across the wood table, gripping the heavy mug until her knuckles turned white. "What about you? How long since you cared?"

He slammed his palms down, pushed back in the chair, and stalked out, leaving the half-drunk coffee spilling off the edge. She watched him go, listened to the tractor's throaty crank and steady rumble as he chugged toward the plowing.

She had challenged Amos again. The first time, she felt frightened. Suppose he took to violence? He often jabbed the pigs or flogged the goats when he handled them. He even switched the cow for not moving fast enough. Only the bull escaped his harshness. As time went by, she realized he would not hit her, but knew he felt nothing about belittling and calling her names. *Does he feel anything for me? Contempt? Partnership?*

Within a week, the kitten gained strength and lapped milk on its own. It followed her around the house and purred whenever she held it on her lap. Late afternoons, her chores completed, she sat in the porch rocker and waited for Amos to come in from the fields, sometimes dozing as the sunlight faded. The kitten snuggled against her bosom, its tiny purr a sweet vibration.

Asleep in the porch chair Wednesday, she did not hear Amos until he bellowed and slammed through the pasture gate, leaving it banging back and forth against the corner post.

"I told you to keep the bull from the cows, you dimwitted cunt!"

"Last Thursday you said. The Pole was not to have had cows in the pasture today." She stood quickly, holding the kitten. The chair teetered violently and crashed over sideways.

Frightened with the harsh commotion, the kitten grabbed at Udean's dress collar with needle claws. Gently she untangled it, sat it inside the kitchen, and faced Amos.

His jaw set and eyes narrowed, he wheeled toward the old barn. She followed.

"He has injured himself butting across the boards to get them cows." Shoulders rigid with anger, Amos stomped into the dank interior, found a rope and wooden prod. He pushed her against the stall divider and raised his fist.

She flinched and turned her head from the threatened blow. None came. Slowly, she swiveled back and faced him.

"Damn you! The sheriff fetched me from the bar in front of every man-jack there." His voice rose and he slammed the rope against the doorframe. "The bull ruined the fencing. Now, I'll have to fork out repair money."

"The bull is dangerous." Her voice rose firm. "The dog set up a barking, then began yelping pitifully. By the time I ran there, the bull had mashed him into a lifeless pulp in the grass." She stared at him, her face white, eyes glassy.

"The dog must have tormented him." Amos spit the words between clenched teeth.

"No. The bull was mad to get at the heifers. The dog ran between them. The man also ran between." She stood facing Amos. Her voice trembled. "I called the sheriff."

"You? You are to blame?" His eyes bulged. "The sheriff can order my bull sold to slaughter. Is that what you want?"

"Be grateful your neighbor is alive. Otherwise there'd be the devil to pay."

"Damn you to hell. We shall see." He stalked across the yard, throwing words back against her. "I'll fetch the bull home."

Udean nodded. Her back straight, she turned and stumbled into the house, legs unsteady. Her stomach knotted and a bile taste rose in her mouth. She picked up the kitten and cradled it against her neck, the tiny creature attempting to hide in her hair.

By the time Amos led the bull home and penned it, night had dragged the sun beneath the horizon and obscured the farm. She heard him gather his fencing tools and materials, toss them in the pickup, and rattle off.

She went to bed late and slept restless, holding the kitten in the crook of her arm. Although she listened for Amos most of the night, she did not hear the door slam or bedsprings creak. She finally dozed just as a water-pale light filtered across the sky. The speckled rooster crowed, formally announcing morning.

When she entered the kitchen, she found Amos sitting on the screen porch, elbows propped on his knees, hands cradling his head. The kitten followed her and sat quietly beneath the table.

She measured grounds for the coffee, grateful for the mellow brown aroma that filled the kitchen as it brewed. Finished, she poured two mugs and stepped out onto the porch. Translucent steam rose from the liquid, floated briefly, and disappeared. Amos took the mug offered and held it in his rough paw.

"That hired man told me." He sat utterly still. "He ran out to help and saw the bull had killed the dog. He said it would have done the Polack in had you not heard the racket and run in front with the shovel." Amos shook his head. "He said it's good you are stout. You swung the shovel with two hands and smashed the bull on the nose. Had it not been for the nose ring, you could not have stopped him. The Pole's boy dragged his father away."

Udean sat in the wooden rocker and stared straight ahead, feeling the tension radiate off Amos. She sipped her coffee. The kitten crawled into her lap and sat, without purring, green eyes watchful.

"That fool foreigner put his young heifers out." Amos gritted his teeth. "Now we have both suffered because of his stupidity."

She did not respond but laced her fingers around the warm cup.

"You always protect those around you." Amos spoke slow and soft. "The goats when I grew too rough. The cow. Even the hogs. I thought you weak."

"I know." Udean nodded and stared into his sun-leathered face.

"You have been a hard worker. A solid wife."

"I chose you and this life. We have built our time together." She watched his face soften. "If only we had cared beyond the dead babies."

"No sense counting out regrets. What's done can't be remade."

"I once loved you Amos." She stilled the rocker. "We have survived and built a life here with our animals and neighbors. Now we grow old together."

"I think, for some of our years, I loved you." He stood stiffly. "The bull has to be sold."

She did not reply.

Hesitantly, he stretched his hand toward her and touched her hair so lightly she thought perhaps she imagined it.

"I could have lost everything." He swallowed hard, his Adam's apple bobbing. He placed the half-drunk coffee on a ledge next to the door. "Keep the kitten. It'll make a fine cat." He pushed the screen door open, and walked to the tractor shed, leaving a trail in the early dew.

She rocked. Her chair creaked, an alto accompaniment to the twittering sparrows. She closed her eyes and listened to the joyful chorus.

The Soldier and the Lady

He slept in fits and starts most of the night. In Beaumont, he got off the Greyhound and used the public toilet. Afterwards, he finished a cigarette and flicked it away. He ran a calloused hand across a puckered scar high on his cheekbone in a slow gesture of weariness.

Driver announced 'all board' and watched as the man found his seat again. When the last passenger got on, the driver closed the doors with a pneumatic belch.

Beyond sleep, the soldier watched as night dissolved and billboards, suspended in morning mist, declared "Welcome to Louisiana." He stared out at piney woods, algae-coated swamp, and palmetto scrubland gliding past the windows. Occasionally a lone oil pump punctuated the jumble.

By full daylight, the bus hiccupped into Lake Charles in a cloud of diesel fumes.

"Everybody off. Rest stop while we wait on the east-bound hound." The driver glanced in the mirror at his passengers, then limped off, stiff from hours behind the wheel.

The soldier stood and stretched, arching his back, then buttoned his drab green uniform and stepped off the bus into the mid-morning humidity. Been a time when he felt high on pride at the uniform and the unit patches. He had left that in Nam. The familiar signs of a headache started across his shoulders and crept up his neck.

"Where can I get something to eat?"

"Restaurant cross the highway over yonder." The driver jerked his thumb toward a diner with a sun-warped sign creaking in the wind.

The soldier acknowledged the comment with a nod, replaced his hat, and settled it low to block the sun. He stood a moment in the shade of the terminal and lit a cigarette. His headache burst full blown behind his eyes.

Wind gusted and chased plastic bags down the street until they snagged on a weed or around a parking meter to flutter like small scraps of memory. He crunched across the gravel lot and stood outside the restaurant window. A faded, handwritten placard advertised 'Breakfast Served Anytime.' He stubbed the half-smoked cigarette into a pot of dead petunias and pulled the door open.

Inside, a window air conditioner coughed intermittently, struggling to cool the muggy diner. Cooking odors billowed out of the kitchen. An anemic-looking busboy clattered dishes into a plastic tub, playing background to the hum of conversation. The boy stopped and watched the soldier with something like envy. Sporadically, a service bell tinkled.

"Sit anywhere, sweetie." The waitress, thin and sharp, hollered over the restaurant din. "I get you in a minute."

He nodded, took a booth near the window, and studied the ketchup-speckled menu. He lit another cigarette and squinted through the slow curl of smoke.

One coffee refill later, the waitress set eggs swimming in grease before him. He had dreamed of two over easy, toast, and ham during his years in the jungle. He stared at the plate, no longer hungry, and wondered why he had ordered.

He smelled the woman before she shuffled to a stop next to his booth. He glanced up into exhausted eyes and Medusa hair around a sagging face. Another damaged soul.

"You going to eat that?" She stood next to the table without expression and nodded toward the eggs.

He glanced down at the food.

"I'm not begging or asking for charity. I'm offering to eat it rather than have it go to waste. Cook throws it in the dumpster. Stuff like that draws rats and stray cats." Her voice had a nasal quality.

He pushed the plate away and motioned toward the opposite side of the booth.

"I don't reckon I'm eating it after all. Sit."

With dignity, she placed an array of shopping bags under the table, pulled off fingerless gloves, slipped out of a threadbare coat, and sat. She nodded toward him and ate slow, taking the time to taste each bite.

He gestured for a refill and an extra cup for the woman.

The waitress, face pinched with disapproval, held the glass pot slightly away from the table. "Who's paying for this, sweetie?"

The woman stared into the plate, grime-encrusted fingers frozen on the fork. She sat perfectly still, waiting.

"I'll pay." He nodded toward the cup. "Bring her some water too."

They sat in silence. He smoked. She ate.

Finished, she sopped the toast around the plate for the last egg yolk smear and redeye gravy, dabbed her fingers clean, and placed the knife and fork across the plate.

"Thank you, Corporal. Saves the garbage men." She pushed out of the booth.

"No need to waste things." He smiled at her, crushed the last of his cigarette.

"I had a boy once. He volunteered. Might be you could have seen him. Gone now."

"Lotta boys didn't come back. You're a good mother to keep remembering."

"Thank you." She stared at him. Shuffling away on post-thick legs, she ignored the other customers.

He finished his coffee, disregarding whispered comments the next booth over.

"You need a refill, honey?" The waitress waltzed by with two pots.

"No, thanks." He stood and placed several crumpled bills on the table. "That should cover everything for me. And the lady."

He stepped into the sodden day. Gnats buzzed around his ears. He swatted at them indifferently. The whir of traffic and growl of Jake brakes throbbed toward him. The day showed signs of climbing into triple-digit heat.

He watched the old lady disappear down the sidewalk, her back straighter and shuffle gone.

Home, a few hours away, seemed less daunting.

Dear Sis,

Cousin Gussie and I have danced our feet off at a street festival in Nashville. They actually closed the street and set up barricades. Can you believe something so old fashioned? This is the place for music and men. Next time you HAVE to come with me.

Luv, Angie

Saturday Night Street Festival

You hear the band crank up, twang out the first tune, and warm up. Heavy on the drum, rhythm guitar pulsing into the humidity. *Hot damn.*

Street closed off, asphalt radiating heat, fountain throwing water droplets catching the last light. Late afternoon that's gonna stomp into the evening. Too far back to get a good look, but you know somebody's dancing wearing a straw cowboy hat, cream colored with a narrow black band—the kind that comes from any western wear outlet.

You push through the crowd, do your own hip action as you gyrate toward the stage, music vibrating in your head. You shuffle and do a hand flutter and shoulder roll. Ease on over into the fringe of the crowd, jiving, feeling good.

Two male dancers in a circle of onlookers got it going. You spot the cowboy hat, faux pearl snaps on a blue shirt. He's prancing with a man in a baseball cap wearing a Harley-Davidson tee. You take in the smiles, notice the fellers sweating bullets, slick with the heat. Lordy, you lose yourself in that raucous beat.

Cowboy got a small head, broad flat hands, and short neck. Tee-shirt's chubby with a beer pot and ruddy face.

They got moves incongruous with their doughboy appearances. Did you ever see anyone so flexible? Doing the bump, knocking hips 'cause it's done that way. Girls off to the side can't keep up.

Line dance getting started. You *feel* it. Slide, slide, step back, cross leg bend, kick, spin and slide, slide, kick. Yee-haw.

Honky-tonk delight from that guitar picker, seamless and fine. Tee-shirt, a little awkward, snatches the lead from Cowboy, catches the groove, hips swiveling. They hustle with heads bobbing side-to-side and feet stomping, keeping time. Hands grasp, slide down the arm, do a pass-under, swing out and back in a round strut. Fingers jabbing air, acting sassy, doing a one-foot spin.

Band sits back, cools down, takes a break. You finish your beer and watch while Cowboy approaches the stage, got a song request. Lead guitarist smiles, nods, gives a fist bump.

Barefoot children splash through the fountain and shake strings of wet hair like dogs. Squeals jump sparkling into the air. Evening sun starts down.

Second set. Acoustic guitar got the melody line for Johnny Cash 'Ring of Fire.' You throw your head back when the keyboard mimics that trumpet call and glide up front with your flatfoot Texas Two-Step on display, strutting your best kicker moves. Your country soul *knows* this rhythm, snatched vibrating from the poor side of town.

Third set starts to loop. Ropes of street light pop on and shove night aside. Air perfumed with beer, cotton candy, and hot dogs with kraut. Street barriers hold the delight, life abandoned to the moment.

You laugh right out loud. Cowboy and Tee-shirt still working it. Folks lounging on the side. You can't be no better place. Summertime. Street festival. Dancing.

Ads for Mule Feed

Harold Williams pressed his face against the window, cupped his eyes against the glare and drew back to read the Green Country Garden and Feed Supply ad again. His hands shook as he stuffed the paper into his overalls pocket. *Nothing risked, nothing gained.*

He opened the feed store door. Dust motes drifted through the air. He waited next to a stack of bagged topsoil and shifted from one to foot to the other while a bald man finished with several customers. Harold felt acutely aware of his own unwashed body odor.

"Sir? Mister?" Harold started in a high tinny voice, cleared his throat and started over. "I come to see y'all got any work here."

"What makes you think I've got work?"

"I seen your mule feed ad in the *Harrison Daily* and that give me the idea of coming by."

The man pulled his glasses off, crossed his arms and leaned against the wooden counter. "People around here are buying miniature mules so the ad lets them know we're carrying feed. That ad didn't say anything about a job."

"It give me the idea though." Harold glanced down and scuffed his boot toe along the floor. "I'm used to hard work and I know mules. Maybe, I could work a day or two. Sort of try out. You can decide if I do good enough to keep on with pay."

"I see. You don't look strong enough to work. In fact, looks to me like you haven't had a good meal in some time." He cocked his head to the side and eyed the worn boot held together with duct tape.

Harold felt his courage spiral down some distant drain.

"I'm naturally a bit boney. Ma says I take after the old man." He straightened up, goaded by an unseen hand. "Since he took off, me and her barely making ends meet. We done hung on 'bout as long as we can."

"What's your name?"

"Harold Williams. Folks call me Hal."

"I see." He scratched his head. "I'm the owner here—Glenn Turner—Elijah is my man in the back. He fills customer orders and loads whatever is necessary. I don't need anybody."

"Yes, sir, but I need the work. I'll stay too. Not quit on you."

Turner tapped his pencil on several Purina brochures next to the cash register. "What happened to your last job?"

"I got hired as janitor at the high school. It were a temporary job while the regular feller out on surgery. He come back and I been looking ever since. Hard to find work here."

"Yeah. Not much around." Turner rubbed the back of his neck, put his pencil down, and then picked it up again.

"With summer rush coming on, I guess I can give you a try." He sighed and shook his head. "Start now. We'll talk about pay after I see how you do. Tomorrow, when you come back, be sure you've washed. You smell ripe."

The front bell tinkled. A woman entered the store, ambled up and down the aisles, and stopped to inspect vegetable plants. Finally, she selected a pair of garden gloves, fumbled for her billfold, and turned toward the counter.

"Go on out to the warehouse." Turner gestured toward the back. "Elijah will show you what to do. He'll have the final word as to how you work out." He shifted toward the customer with a smile. "How can I help?"

When Glenn Turner arrived the next morning, Hal sat on the top step near the front door, hair still wet and dressed in faded jeans. Too large, he had scrunched them secure around his waist with a knotted belt.

Keys jangling, Glenn unlocked the door, flipped the sign to 'Open,' and turned on lights. "Glad to see you came back. Go on out to the loading dock and warehouse. Elijah comes in about this time. You do what he says."

"Yes, sir." Hal nodded and shifted awkwardly from one foot to another.

As if on cue, Elijah appeared on the dock, his black face split in a smile. He moved with the deliberate grace of a man accustomed to physical work. He hung his jacket on a corner peg, pushed the heavy sliding door along its track, and threw the cavernous area open to a pale morning light. Sparrows twittered and swooped along the rafters. Pigeons strutted across the dock, cooing.

Hal stepped inside the warehouse, took a deep breath, and exhaled slow, savoring the scent of molasses-laced mule feed and chicken pellets.

"Well, young feller, you ready to get to work?" Elijah pulled on a pair of leather gloves and nodded toward a flat-bed truck growling into the parking lot.

"That be Mr. Hawkins with hay Mr. Glenn done ordered. We unload and stack it in yonder shed. We got a busy day ahead."

The two barely finished stacking hay when a landscape service contractor and several farmers arrived. Hal wiped sweat off his forehead with his arm and glanced up to see Elijah grin at him.

"Already hot, ain't it?"

"Yes, sir, Mr. Elijah. It heated up right smart."

They both laughed and bent to carry feed, top soil, and fertilizer bags out for customers.

During an early afternoon lull, Glenn strolled back to the warehouse.

"Elijah, you bring any lunch today?"

"Yes, suh. My missus fixed me up ham biscuits."

"Hal, what about you?"

"No, sir, Mr. Turner. I'll work on through. Ma fix me up come evening when I get home." He grinned.

"Well, you worked hard yesterday and have stayed busy this morning. Like we agreed, you're on temporary tryout two days, but I feel I owe you something." Glenn, hands shoved in his khakis, gave Hal a speculative look. "Come on across the street to the Burger Barn and I'll buy you lunch."

"It ain't necessary to buy me no lunch." Hal wiped sweat off his face, smiled shyly, and wiped his hands down the jeans.

"I'll feel better if you accept."

Glenn Turner held the Burger Barn door open for Hal and gestured him inside. A young woman stood across the counter engrossed in *Photoplay and TV Mirror*. Valerie according to her name tag. She did not look up nor offer to help.

The two men, heads craned up, scanned the menu posted above the pass-through.

"Valerie, suppose you put that magazine down, take our orders, then you can read." Glenn dug in his hip pocket and laid out a ten. "Hal is working at the store today and needs lunch."

She rolled her eyes, popped her Juicy Fruit twice, and slid the magazine aside. Pulling a pencil from behind her ear, she stood poised over the order pad.

"I'll have fries, a cheese burger, and a cup of coffee." Glenn nudged Hal with an elbow and gestured him forward.

"What will you take?" Without looking up, she popped her gum, and continued writing the first order.

"I'll take some fries, a hamburger, and a cherry coke." Hal, face flushed warm, stammered. "Please, ma'am."

"What size?"

"Give Hal a large on everything. I'll take a regular," Glenn spoke brusquely.

"Here or to go?" She popped her gum again.

"We need everything to go."

Valerie rang the order up, collected the burgers from the cook, drew the drinks, and shoved everything across the counter.

Glenn took a bag and passed the other with the cherry coke along to Hal. Glenn dumped two sugars in his coffee. "Thank you."

Valerie stared at Hal. "Do I know you?"

"No." Hal felt his ears grow hot again.

"Well then, you can stop staring. Put your eyeballs back in your head." She slid her magazine to center counter, licked her forefinger, and flipped the page over.

The two men ambled out of the Barn, crossed the street, and strolled back to the store.

"Have you met Valerie before?"

"Not exactly. She was in the grade right behind me." Hal fumbled with his drink. "I done poorly in school. Plus that's about the time Pap took off. I dropped out. She never noticed me."

Glenn Turner grunted a response as he stomped up the steps and pulled the feed store door open.

• • •

Valerie Johnson lived with her mother in a prefab single-wide. Situated on the south side near the wheel plant, the trailer sat balanced on concrete blocks, with room underneath for stray cats and spiders.

Barely seventeen, she donned flip-flops with plastic yellow flowers and minced around town carrying her brown Chihuahua, Princess, whenever off work.

Her mother, the reigning town floozy, tried to teach Valerie what she called "womanly tricks." Valerie shrugged her off, saying she planned on a movie career as soon as she could save up bus money for Hollywood. Besides she reasoned, she needed a respectable job. Her mother countered with "respectable don't pay bills."

• • •

Six months later, Hal arrived at the store and announced he had turned eighteen. Glenn and Elijah clapped him on the back and shook hands.

"Lord he'p us. Man grow'd." Elijah beamed and shook hands again. "Happy Birthday."

"You're old enough to vote. Congratulations. Happy Birthday." Glenn pulled his glasses off and smiled.

Harold shifted from one foot to the other. "You and Mr. Elijah been good to me. But, I'm on my own now." Tears pooled in his eyes.

"Oh?" Glenn put his glasses on again. "What happened to your mother?"

"Ma say she worn out. Say she go up to Minnesota to live with her second cousin. I don't reckon I'll ever see her again." He wiped his nose on his shirtsleeve.

"I'm sorry to hear this. You think you'll be okay?"

Elijah stood silent.

"Ma say I'm old enough to take care of my own self, now I'm turned eighteen." Hal stared down at his feet. "She done took the welfare check and left. Told me be careful and send in rent fifth of the month. Said she hated to leave me on my own." He coughed and shook his head. "Said she didn't see no other way I miss her already."

"What about your daddy?"

"Well, he never owned up to being my pa. Ma said he was but he never give me his name. He lived with us a spell then lit out. Don't rightly know more than that."

• • •

Alone, Hal lived in a rented room. He managed by wearing rumpled clothes, while he worked full time at the feed store, and ate at the Burger Barn. Always the same meal—double burger, large fries, and cherry coke. He said he went for the cheap food, but truth be told, he went to see Valerie. She never seemed to notice.

• • •

His second year at Green Country, Glenn Turner awarded him fifteen cents an hour raise. Harold bought a new pair of jeans. With the work and burgers, he gradually shed his gangly boyishness.

Occasionally, he dropped by the Barn after the feed store closed and treated himself to a vanilla-strawberry-chocolate triple-dip cone. He sat in a booth, licked his ice cream, and watched Valerie. She sat on a metal stool beside the cash register and read her magazines.

Late one Wednesday, her head snapped up at the customer buzzer. When she saw Hal, she smiled and shoved her magazine aside.

He hesitated by the door.

"Hal, you know how you're always mooning after me?" Valerie handed him an extra-large cone before he even spoke.

"I reckon." He took the cone and counted out exact change.

"Let's go to the drive-in after I get off work Friday." She leaned forward twirling a blonde curl around her finger.

"You and me?"

"Yeah, you and me."

He felt heat climb up his neck. Ice cream dribbled down the cone.

"I always get stuck working late on Fridays." He licked the chocolate curl on top. "The movie might be near over by the time I'd get loose."

"The *Invasion of the Body Snatchers* is on." Valerie rolled her eyes and popped her gum. "That's a good one. Real scary."

"Well, I got no car or nothing."

Her mouth puckered up in a pout. "We take my mama's car. Her and Bill always use his car cause he tells his wife he's out-of-town on business. Anyway, I'm not going to watch the movie."

"You ain't? Why you going? "

"Do I have to spell it out?" She glared at him. A frown wrinkled her forehead. "We're going to be together." She leaned forward and giggled.

"Be together?" He blinked. "What's that supposed to mean?"

"You are such a ninny." She pulled a string of gum from her mouth, licked her lips, and wound it back with her tongue.

Hal's eyes widened. "I never done nothing like this before." Ice cream dripped down the cone and puddled on the counter. He pulled several napkins from the metal dispenser and accidently knocked it sideways. He fumbled, set the holder upright, and stared at her.

• • •

It took four after-hour dates before Valerie could get Hal to finger her sweet spot and another two before she maneuvered him into the full-blown homerun.

Later, Hal practically waltzed into the Burger Barn for his lunch, still grinning and feeling randy.

Valerie shoved his order cross the counter before the door even closed.

"How'd you know what I want?" He grinned at her.

"You so boring you order the same damn thing all the time."

Hal's face fell slack. He cocked his head to the side.

"I got to talk to you. Private like. Meet me out back near the dumpster," she said.

"It smells out there." Harold blinked and gripped the paper sack.

"And that place you work, with all them sweaty farmers and shit, don't smell?" She hissed through clamped teeth. "I said, meet me. What is it you don't understand about that?"

Perplexed, he dug in his pocket for change, pushed it across the counter, gave her a sidelong glance, and stalked out.

By late afternoon, Green Country customers had drifted away to their respective chores. The next rush usually came about six when office workers dropped by on their way home.

With the lull, Hal strode out of the store, crossed the street, and crunched past the drooping marigolds clustered along the concrete wall toward the Barn's dumpster. He rounded the corner and wrinkled his nose at the odor of rotted meat scraps and rancid cooking oil. Clouds of steam and garbled cussing floated through the kitchen's back door screen.

Valerie slammed out the door, lit a Kool, and inhaled deeply. Her hands shook.

"I'm pregnant."

"You mean with a baby?" Hal stuttered.

"Of course with a baby. What do you think, with a puppy?" She thumped ash off her cigarette. "I ain't lying. We need to get married. Right away." She took another drag.

He stared at her, noticing for the first time how her uniform gapped open at the waist.

"Valerie, Sweetie, I don't understand."

"Don't call me Sweetie." Her voice had a peevish quality. "You need to make plans to be taking care of me." Without waiting for a reply, she marched back into the restaurant trailing cigarette smoke.

Shaking his head, Hal shuffled toward the store, face scrunched into worry ridges.

• • •

"Elijah, you a married man. How many times does it take for a woman before she has a baby?"

"Why you ask such a question?" Elijah slung a bag of feed onto a pickup, slammed the tailgate, and signaled the driver. "I figured you too shy to be doing it." He shucked his gloves off and stared at Hal. "Besides, you in them high school make-up classes most nights, right? When you got time be fooling with a woman?"

Hal brushed his hand through his bristly hair and shrugged.

"Well, I been keeping company with Valerie that works across at the Barn. She says she's in a family way."

"You ever done it with her?"

"Yeah. Once. About five days ago."

"Once? Well, I don't recollect nothing baking in the oven rise up that fast." Elijah slapped his gloves on his thigh. "Not after one time. You right certain it's you done got her in a family way?"

"Must be. I ain't heard tell she been with no other feller. Besides, she said so."

"Heard tell? Who you know tell you anyhow?" The man hunkered down on his heels next to a straw bale. "Her mama do it all over town. Apple don't fall far from the tree."

Hal plopped on the dock, legs dangling over the edge and stared at his thick calluses and broken nails.

"Valerie don't act pleased. For certain, I can't let no baby come in this world without taking on her daddy's name."

"Well, I don't know nothing much about that young lady. My guess is she using you."

"Using me?" Hal's eyes widened and he felt heat creep up his neck. "But we *done it*. You don't think she'd lie, do you?"

Elijah cleared his throat. "I don't know but one thing. No man ever know'd for certain if he got a woman in a family way. Woman say it you, then you trust that and do right. Ain't the baby's fault." Elijah stood and walked into the warehouse shadows. "Go talk with Mr. Glenn. He know about stuff like that." He paused and turned back to Hal. "'Course you can always run. Leave her pick another fool."

Hal shook his head. "Would that be right? I kinda think that's what happened to my ma. I hate to think about a baby without a daddy."

"You decide."

• • •

For the next two days, Hal avoided the Burger Barn while he mulled things over and worked up his nerve.

"Mr. Turner, you reckon you could lend me that old rusted truck out back?" Hal had waited until closing on Thursday and now stood with a Farmall cap in hand.

"You can borrow it if you can get it running." Glenn glanced up, then continued totaling receipts. "Needs gas. Where are you planning on going?" He gave the adding machine a final pull and ripped the tape off.

"Over to the courthouse."

"That's on Wabash Street, six blocks over." The man cocked his head to one side. "None of my business, but you can walk there. What's really going on?"

"Valerie Johnson and I plan on getting married. I kinda want to take her some place nice. Maybe Eureka Springs. I seen in the newspaper they have honeymoon specials there." Hal grinned, and then grew solemn.

"That's why I need the truck. I was hoping you could get along without me a few days. I be back by the weekend when work's heavy."

"Married?" Glenn Turner's jaw dropped, his mouth open. "Son, you don't have a place for a wife. A wife is expensive. This job doesn't pay enough." He picked up his half-filled coffee cup, and then sat it down again. "What about your plans for your GED? Maybe college?"

"I got $257 saved up." Hal grinned, buckteeth protruding. "Besides, she's having a baby and I got to do right."

"Baby?" Glenn pulled his glasses off and rubbed the bridge of his nose. "When did you find this out?"

"Two days ago."

"Are you sure it's yours? Seems a little too convenient."

"Elijah says a man never knows whose baby a woman have. He says a feller just trust her and do what's right. If I marry her, it keeps the baby from being a bastard." He shuffled his feet. "Baby needs a daddy and a name. Don't matter to the baby who that is. Do it?"

Glenn closed his mouth.

"Besides, Valerie told me she's not living with me right away." Hal looked up and smiled. "She told me she'd stay at her mama's and for me to stay put. That way I can keep saving up money for us later."

"Not live together? What kind of marriage is that? What does she plan to do with the baby?"

"I'll help her take care of it. We can do it together."

"I'm not in favor of this union." Glenn rubbed his nose again and replaced his glasses. "Especially under the circumstances. I want you to reconsider and think about the long term."

"I'll think on it some more. You not being in favor and all. But that baby don't need to be no bastard. Needs a name. I know I can be a good daddy."

•••

Hal and Valerie married on Monday. The county tax clerk and Valerie's mother, arriving with several wilted daisies, served as witnesses. Afterwards, the clerk shook Hal's hand and wished him good luck. Valerie's mother kissed her on the cheek and swept out as soon as the judge, enveloped in a transparent cloud of Aqua Velva aftershave, made his pronouncement. The old courthouse windows distorted and softened the afternoon light, forming misshaped rectangles on the parquet floors. Hal considered the colors a good sign.

Valerie refused the Eureka Springs wedding night stay, but took the shopping trip. Hal obliged her, saying he might damage the baby if they *did it* while she was pregnant. He followed her from shop to shop until closing and then drove back to Harrison in the dark. Valerie slept the entire trip home, snoring, her mouth open.

Hal wrestled with mixed feelings: He had mooned over Valerie since high school, thinking her especially pretty. Now, here he had married her. Still, he could not quite get his mind around how she got pregnant so fast. He felt uncertain if she even cared about him since she called him Bill three times. The events troubled him.

•••

A scant week had slipped past when Glenn Turner looked up to see a sheriff's car pull into the feed store parking lot.

"Why, Deputy Smith, what brings you out today?" Glenn extended his hand.

"Not much. Just need to see someone by the name of Harold Williams. I understand he works for you."

"Something happen?"

"Well, seems his wife's been assaulted. She's in the emergency room." The sheriff shifted his gun belt and shook his head. "Lady wouldn't say how this happened, just keeps asking for her husband. Seems odd her saying she's pregnant, wants her husband yet lives with her mother and doesn't want to press charges."

• • •

"I lied to you." Valerie began sobbing as soon as Hal entered the room. "I needed to get married because I'm pregnant. It ain't your baby." Her nose dripped. She wiped her hand across her face, smearing snot.

She looked like a sick cat with her protruding belly-lump, black eye, swollen lip, and bruises. Still, a certain sweetness lingered around her.

"Not my baby?" He leaned forward, frowned, and petted her hand.

"I lied, didn't you hear me?"

"What am I supposed to do?" He dropped her hand.

"You are so dense. I don't treat you like a husband. I don't wear that wedding band. You probably got it out of a Cracker Jack box anyway." She paused, then wound up again. "I'm going to Hollywood soon as this baby's born. You get ready to buy my ticket."

"Take care of you? Buy you a bus ticket?" The bed creaked as he shifted and stood. "I don't think I want to stay married, what with you living with your mama and ignoring me." He shoved his hands in his jeans. "And I never got no ring out of no Cracker Jacks neither." He pulled a metal chair up and sat. "I can tell you got some other feller on your mind."

"Maybe I do."

"Why don't you marry him? Why bother me?"

She sat up in bed and pitched a box of Kleenex at him. It bounced off his chest and slid under the bed.

"He's already married you dope. Besides, he don't want to." She snuffed and wiped her eyes. "Mama found out I was pregnant and told me to fix it. That's when I hit on marrying you as a cover up." Valerie coughed and fell into a fresh round of tears. "Last night Mama found out exactly who the father really is."

"Go on. Finish telling." Hal closed his mouth, his lips pressed in a thin line.

"Bill, that married man she's seeing, is the one. He told me he'd get rid of Mama if I let him do me. We been at it for months. Mama found out and threw a hissy fit. Said she'd teach me."

A nurse entered the room, took vital signs, made notes on the chart, and left, trailing a smell of rubbing alcohol.

Valerie buried her face in her hands. "These gossipy nurses probably told everybody Mama beat me. Whole town will know by tonight."

Hal turned and stood near the window. He watched a pickup and several cars leave the parking lot. A van with a family drove in. Kids bounced out and swarmed around while the mother wrestled with a baby and stroller.

"I don't want to spend my life in this hillbilly town with everyone talking. And I sure don't want to live with some skinny mule-headed ridgerunner imbecile." She groped around for something else to throw, gave up, and sobbed into the pillow.

"Mama figures she can get money out of the baby's real daddy. She keep after him and let me stay at her place until the baby arrives as a reminder."

"Not right you call me names and treat me like some throwaway shoe nobody wants." Hal clenched his fists, turned from the window, and stood splay-legged next to the bed. "I can't bear the thought of that baby not having a proper daddy. At least with me and the paperwork, it will have a name."

Valerie blinked. She fell silent.

"I got to get back to work." He marched stiff-leg to the door. "Hospital will take care of you then send you home."

"What am I supposed to do?"

"I don't know." He shoved his hands into his pockets. "I thought I could love you and do right by this baby."

"But I still love him."

"Who?"

"Bill. That other man."

"You married to me. You living off your Mama and she only wanting you around for the money. You got a baby coming. You'd better think about things. I can't wait forever." He pushed out the door and stomped down the corridor.

Hal continued at the feed store. He avoided Valerie.

When a rosy baby girl arrived three months later, Valerie graciously called Hal after she listed him as the father on the birth certificate. In turn, he insisted on naming the baby Eve Josephine after his mother. She did not carry the Williams family hawk-nose. Townspeople nodded knowingly and waited to see what traits might emerge.

Two days later, Hal collected the baby and took her to his rented room. Elijah's wife took care of Eve during the day while Hal worked. He took over at night.

No longer slender enough to fit into her fancy clothes, Valerie nonetheless strolled about town carrying her dog, Princess. She got a job at the Red Rooster Grill, a move up in class she said. Her face took on a drained quality despite the layered-on make-up and eye shadow. She smacked her gum incessantly. Her teeth showed the effects of too much sugar and too little brushing.

Hal completed his high school diploma and, at his teacher's urging, applied at a work-for-tuition college in Missouri. He continued at the feed store until late August.

Glenn gave him the rusted pickup as a graduation-new-beginning-and-baby-gift rolled into one. Hal wired the muffler back underneath, changed the oil, and used a bungee cord to hold the tailgate closed. He didn't bother with the dented fender.

With plans to leave the next morning, he drove straight to Valerie's place. She answered his knock immediately, holding Princess across one arm.

"I done heard you leaving town and taking my baby."

"It's high time you started treating me better. I'm taking *my* little Eve and going away to college. Folks already helped me with plans."

"Your baby?" Valerie hiccupped and began crying. "You nothing but a peckerwood."

"I won't be after I finish college. Besides, since we're legally married, Eve's *my* daughter. Mr. Turner and I talked with his lawyer friend."

She stared dumbfounded.

"You never talked to me like this before."

"I'm a father now. I got responsibilities. I always been a hard worker. I know I can do this."

Eyes wide, she stared at him, plunked down on the steps, sat the dog on the ground, and burst into fresh tears.

Hal squatted before her, but did not touch her nor offer any comfort.

"I'm leaving early tomorrow. You come with us, you gotta act like a wife and mother. You stay here, I'll give you money for a bus ticket to California. You choose. Suit yourself." He stood, strode to his truck, and clanked away.

• • •

Next morning, true to his word, Hal started north out of town toward Missouri. The sleepy community yawned in the tangerine-spiked light and stretched awake.

He stopped at Valerie's trailer. Eve gurgled, kicked, and smiled in a blanket-lined clothesbasket Elijah's wife had fashioned.

Valerie sat on the front door step with Princess. She jumped up when the pickup pulled in, jerked the door open, and plunked the dog in with the baby. Tossing two cardboard boxes in the cargo bed, she scrunched into a sliver of seat. Unwrapping a stick of Juicy Fruit, she stuffed it in her mouth.

Princess, ears pricked forward, sat paws on the basket rim. Occasionally, she licked the baby's face and wagged her ratty tail. Eve giggled.

On his way to the store, Glenn saw the pickup rattle north through the traffic light. Reba McEntire's new hit on KOOL 94.3 radio blared as Hal drove by, tapping the steering wheel in time to the music.

He remembered the first day Harold Williams—a skinny, nervous boy—walked into the Green Country Garden and Feed Supply store. A boy no longer, Hal drove out of town a man.

Glenn whooped aloud, slapped his leg, and made a mental note to place an ad for mule feed. Maybe he'd get lucky and another bright fellow might ask for a job.

Elijah would be glad for the help.

One Dollar and a Red Button

The moan of the midnight freight woke Tom. The lone-some wail coiled around his grief, strangling him. He pant-ed for air.

Drenched with sweat, he rolled over, swung his feet off the side of the bed, and sat on the edge. Night dreams about Helen again. He leaned over to his nightstand, picked up his Marlboros, thumped one out, and held it unlit between his teeth.

No sense trying to sleep. Might as well get up and make coffee.

Details flashed before him. His hand trembled, spilling coffee grounds on the floor.

Helen got killed August 10 when the afternoon freight plowed over her at the town crossing. Engineer sat down on the whistle a split second before he slammed into that Ford Fairlane and carried her into eternity.

Tom still saw the patrol car as it eased down his drive-way, remembered how the sun glinted off the hood, how Bugle's deep hound bawl announced visitors, then how Preacher Johnson and Sheriff Moore got out. They walked up slow-like, reluctant.

Gravel cut his knees when he sank to the ground and sobbed with raw emotion, cradling his head in both hands. Sheriff removed his hat, shuffled around, and glanced at Preacher. The man clasped his hands and mumbled platitudes, then fell silent.

Weeks later, after the funeral, Kyle Hicks and Leroy Simmons had dropped by. Everyone sat on the porch while Ella Mae, the housemaid, served them sweet iced tea.

"Tom, both of us real sorry about your wife." Leroy twisted his gnarled hands and stared off into the distance.

"You see, we was sitting on that bench on the depot platform, whittling." Kyle paused long enough to put a dip of Copenhagen in his lip. "She was in that there blue car. Done stopped at the cross bars, but them boxcars on that siding musta blocked her from seeing that freight."

"Bam!" Leroy slammed his fist into his palm. "Train hit her and started dragging everything down the tracks. All you seen was a crumpled up mess." He stopped a moment, and then continued. "I called the sheriff and the firefighters. They all come a screaming out to the wreck. That reporter from the *Hamilton County Record* come and took pictures.

"Still, you know, there was something kinda odd—jerky-like—about the way she got on them tracks." Kyle's voice stayed low. He elbowed Leroy. "What'd you think?"

Tom leaned forward, eyes wide. "What do you mean 'odd' and 'jerky'?" He swallowed twice, Adam's apple jerking.

Leroy spat a stream of tobacco juice off the porch. "Well, it were like she didn't really mean to go." He took the John Deere cap off and wiped his bald head.

"Maybe the car stalled. But it kinda seemed like she got pushed." Kyle spoke slow, measuring each word. "I thought I seen a grey truck or something big behind her, but by the time the train got on by and all the screeching ended, there was nothing there. I never could be certain."

"Car got mashed like a tin can," Leroy replaced his cap.

Tom leaned back. He stared off, eyes glazed over. His wife had been a hardcore civil rights activist. She had taken on the school board and town establishment more than once over the years. The community walked a cautious line between generations-deep prejudice and basic human dignity. Ten years before, President Johnson and his Great Society had made folks in Georgia come face-to-face with the issue of skin color. The community still chafed.

Silent on the issue of race, Tom had felt an acute sense of guilt that he allowed Helen to shoulder that burden alone. Chief comptroller for the St. Regis Paper Company, he toiled in a hotbed of good old boys and thinly disguised threats.

His boss, Bo Watkins jabbed at Tom with racist jokes and barbed references to agitators saying, "Folks need to know their place and stay in it." He stared directly at Tom. "Don't matter who it is, ever body can be handled one way or another."

After the funeral, Tom, bereft, spent most of his time in a rocking chair on the back porch. Bugle sat with him, except when he bayed announcing another tuna casserole delivery. Women neighbors, anxious in their Christian duty, dropped off sympathy, pies, and deviled eggs. They checked on Ella Mae, saying she should "keep up with her duties" even with Helen gone.

"Yes, Missus," said Ella Mae. "I'll keep an eye on Mr. Tom and keep Miss Helen's house up good. My boy Jackson helping too. He doing yard work." Such times, Ella Mae's graceful hands took a proffered casserole, nodded graciously, and kept an impassive face.

One morning, still drowning in inertia, Tom saw Bo Watkins stride around the corner of the house. Bo stood before the porch, his spacious girth blocking the entire walkway and bottom step.

"Tom, we got another man to take over your work," Watkins did not mince words or niceties. "Company got to move on. I ain't firing you—what with the circumstances and all—but changes need making." He fumbled in his pocket, pulled out a folded document, and spread it before Tom.

"Sign right here." He clicked a ballpoint and handed it across.

"What's this mean?" Tom felt befuddled, like waking from a bad dream.

"The company's done give you a six-week leave. No pay, but we'll hold the job temporary till you get yourself straight. I'll make a decision later for the company about what to do with you."

Hand trembling, Tom held the paper and squinted at the typed lines.

A final retribution for Helen's politics. A guilty slap for not openly supporting her. A yellow nail in my casket of grief.

He rose and stumbled inside. The screen door slapped closed behind him. He clamped his hands over his ears in a vain attempt to shut out Bo's boom. He felt nauseous.

"Sign the goddamn paper." Bo's voice bounced off Tom's slumped shoulders and retreating back. "Company only got so much patience. Make it easy on yourself. "

• • •

"Mr. Tom you can't go on like this." Ella Mae stood before him, hands on hips, voice ringing with authority. "Me and you get in Miss Helen's office and fix her school materials and clean up her notes. Then we work on her sewing supplies." She hustled down the hall. "There be other folks can use this stuff. We gonna face this together. Come on now. You needs to keep moving. Can't lay down and quit."

He had been proud of Helen. The only history teacher at the Jasper Public High School, she had taught the Civil War. Both sides—Robert E. Lee and Ulysses S. Grant. He knew Helen touched on other facts to challenge her students. Like the exploits of Buffalo Soldiers, named by the Indians for their nappy hair, and their roles after the Civil War, protecting the giant Sequoyah trees in California.

They had sat together, outlining her unit on the 332nd Fighter Group, 'Redtails' out of Tuskegee, fighting home country prejudice and the Nazis. He smiled at how deftly she assigned book reports. Her politics pricked consciences. Some folks said she betrayed her own kind.

"Mr. Tom, you bear on up. Miss Helen not be wanting you to give up. She never stop." Ella Mae's voice lost its gentle edge, took on a roughness.

He felt guilt at his complicity.

"That new teacher high school they hired gonna need these here things. Bless her soul, she got a hard row to hoe with them white trash." Hustling about, Ella Mae stacked files and books, systematically weeding through the room.

Two weeks later, Ella Mae, with Tom silently watching, finished sorting the teaching materials, the boxed papers and books ready for delivery to the new teacher.

The following Monday she waded into the sewing room. Tom trailed behind.

"Your Helen loved to sew. We get this stuff sorted out. Give some of it to the Senior Center over to south side."

Ella Mae's slow accent acted like a salve to Tom's conscience. "Jackson, you come in here and tote out this heavy stuff." She pointed at a stack of boxes and directed her son as if on a field campaign.

A quiet shadow, Jackson had lounged on the porch and waited until his mother called. He backed the dented pickup close to the porch and loaded books, class papers, and sewing supplies.

Twice Tom sat down and sobbed. Ella Mae and Jackson acknowledged his grief then stepped around him.

At the end of the day, with the room almost clear, Ella Mae handed Tom a tin painted with purple forget-me-nots. He opened the box and stared down at loose buttons, a treasure trove of colors and shapes.

"You keep these here buttons, 'cause they pretty," said Ella Mae. "Miss Helen always saying, never know when you be needing an extry button."

She picked up two quilts she had placed aside. "You take these here quilts too. This here her favorites. That one called 'Double Wedding Rings.'" She pointed to a quilt with interlocking purple, red, and lime green circles. "That one 'Sunbonnet Sue.' I think her and her mama pieced them for her hope chest before she married you. You use them come a cold night."

Emotionally exhausted, Tom nodded, took the proffered items, and lovingly stroked the precise stitches, the warm colors. He shuffled down the hall to their old bedroom, tears blurring his steps, and closed the door.

• • •

Tom resigned his position at the mill. Within the year, he sold the Colonial-style house on Ash Street and moved south to Steinhatchee, a fishing community on the Florida coast.

Jackson tagged along. "Keep you company," he said.

Once there, Tom opened a bait shop selling minnows, crickets, canned goods, and tackle. The clapboard building sat on the end of the marina wharf, partially hanging over Apalachee Bay. A rusted tin roof shaded the side porch with its old-fashioned hand pump that pulled brackish bay water to the gut table.

Coloreds and whites alike patronized the shop, first come, first served. After all, Tom reasoned, Jesus hung out with fishermen. It was, therefore, the Christian thing to do, to sell to anyone regardless of color. He felt a need to appease his conscience for not openly supporting Helen.

The bait store opened mornings before the sun yawned awake. Folks with homemade bamboo poles sauntered into the dilapidated building, bought live bait, and ambled out, focused on mullet in tidal creeks near the river's mouth. Intent on redfish and grouper, the rod-and-reel boat crowd arrived as the sky turned from grey to tangerine.

Further along the marina, tourists and church groups climbed aboard the deep-sea rigs that lined the wharf. Pickups belching smoke sat next to sleek Blazers. The throaty chug of boats churning out to sea drifted across the slips.

• • •

Several years after his move, Tom ambled out to the cold drink machine and popped the door open with his passkey.

"You want something to drink? Cool you off?" He gestured with the canned drink. "It's going to be a scorcher today."

"Well, it's not beer but I take it." Jackson smiled, teeth flashing and face gleaming with sweat.

Tom grabbed two Cokes and slammed the door shut.

Gutting and scaling fish, a gore-flecked smelly task, was another service the store offered along with the bait and grocery sales. Jackson earned good tips, especially from the high rollers returning from deep-sea fishing. Mostly he lived on wages and sent his tip money back to Ella Mae. Tom appreciated the way the man sauntered among tourists nonchalantly, treating everyone—belligerent rich and scratch-and-spit crackers—alike.

For his part, he served as an invisible pipeline between the white and black communities along the coast as well as a news conduit back home.

"My Helen relished these humid days. Can you believe that? She said sweat made her feel alive." Tom stood on the store stoop and watched traffic creep past. "You know she never threw a button away. I've kept her old tin with me."

"What makes you think of something like that right now?"

"I don't know. Maybe the heat. Maybe because I found a button in the parking lot this morning. The thing still has thread in the holes." He tossed the button to Jackson who caught it deftly and turned it over in his hand.

Before Jackson could respond, a grey Blazer crunched across the coquina shell parking area. A man got out, Budweiser in hand. His thin companion swung out of the passenger side, walked to the back, and helped pull out an oversize ice chest. They lounged a moment against the vehicle swilling beer.

Tom's stomach knotted. *Bo Watkins. My old boss. Damn. Of all the small-minded, mean people to show up down here.*

Heart thumping, he rose from his chair and faded into the semi-light of the store, turned and watched through the screen door.

Together the men carried the container to the stoop and slammed it down. Sweating, Bo crossed the plank boards, shirt plastered against his fleshy folds.

"Boy, put a rush on these here fish." He gestured with his beer. "We're in a hurry. Need to get on back upstate before dark."

Jackson, with the purposeful attention of a duck after a bug, ambled over and peered into the chest.

"Y'alls got a big mess of fish here." He scratched his nappy hair. "I be glad to fix these here fish up if Mr. Tom say do them. Rights now they's other folks ahead of you."

"Oh yeah? I don't see anybody waiting. You get started like I told you. I'll settle up with this here 'Mr. Tom.' Where the hell is he?"

The booming voice filtered through the screen. Tom's ears rang. His vision blurred. He willed his head to stop spinning.

"Goddamn. If it ain't Tom Whitney." Bo bellowed as he stomped into the store. "In the flesh, as I live and breathe. I heard you crawled off down here after what happened to your wife."

Tom crossed his arms and leaned on the cash register. "Bo Watkins, I haven't seen you since I left the plant."

"Yeah. Imagine that." Bo snorted and stood splay-legged near the counter. "You own this worm trap?" He glanced around the store and smirked.

"Yeah, this is my place. What are doing down here? This is a long way from Jasper."

"Vacation. Wanted to do some real fishing. Didn't figure you'd be 'Mr. Tom.' Kinda ironic, ain't it?"

"What can I do for you?" His mouth dry, Tom swallowed repeatedly. Pressure mounted behind his eyes and his legs trembled.

"Me and my friend need to get on up to Orlando before dark." Bo drained his beer. He crushed the can and sat it on the counter. "We're staying at a motel up there before we drive back to Jasper." He belched. "You tell your nigger to take care of our fish first. You know, for old time's sake." He winked.

Tom struggled to keep his voice even.

"Well, now, Bo, seeing how it's you, I'll do that." Bile rose in his throat, his knees steadied. "But there's an extra charge for any rush order."

"That right? And how much is this rush order?" Bo's eyes narrowed into slits.

"It's posted right up there." Tom pointed at a chalkboard hanging from the ceiling. "'Course, I'll have to charge a bit more than what's posted."

"Yeah? Why's that?"

"You'll need dry ice and separate plastic bags for the fish. Health Department regulations. They're pretty strict about those things."

"Ain't never heard nothing about any regulations."

"Well, it's Florida. They're different down here." He shrugged, careful to keep his face blank.

"You son-of-a-bitch," said Bo. "Old times don't count for nothing with you, do they?"

"Yes, yes they do." Tom glared at Bo. "I'm waiving the guts disposal fee. Want me to tell Jackson go ahead? Move you to the head of the line?" Tom waited, hand resting on the cash register.

Bo stared at Tom, then nodded. The ding of the register twirled in the air between them.

"Jackson usually gets an extra tip for rush work." Tom slid the drawer open. "You can give it to him in person."

Bo's mouth twitched and his Adam's apple bobbed several times. "Tell me, that nigger's tip part of Health Department regulations too?"

He shoved a beefy hand in his shirt pocket, pulled out a wad of money, peeled off the necessary bills, and tossed them toward Tom.

"Me and my friend going across the road to that cafe." Bo jerked his head toward the small building. "We get finished eating, them damn fish better be ready. Wrapped. Individually. With dry ice."

He stalked out the door, stopping long enough to drop a wet, sweat-stained dollar in a watery pool of fish blood before Jackson.

"Your tip." Bo's belly protruded through a gap in his shirt.

His face impassive, Jackson wiped the filet knife on a nubby towel, picked up a grouper, and began work. "Yes, sir." He concentrated, a thin smile playing along his lips.

• • •

Several weeks later, gutting a mess of fish, Jackson glanced sideways at Tom.

"You ever have need of a granny woman?"

"Granny woman? Not sure I know what you mean."

"They womens that conjure things. You know, they study on people and puzzle things into being. They makes stuff happen."

"Like what?"

"Well, they's sort of like witches only they ain't. They can cause spells if they have something from a person."

"Spells? Dark magic?" Tom raised a questioning eyebrow.

"Naw. Not exactly. More like they catch thoughts and feelings from a person and twist them into a knot. Like, if you wished something, the granny conjure it true, make it happen."

"All that mojo sounds a bit strange to me."

"Yes, sir. It do sound strange. You needs think them thoughts real strong before anything happen."

"I've got strong feelings but I'm not sure they include magic."

• • •

On Wednesday, Tom arrived at the store predawn. Bugle, leaning out the truck window, bristled and growled. Tom put a hand on the hound, stepped out of the pickup, and started toward the building.

"Dog ain't gonna hurt me is he?" hollered a disembodied voice.

Tom jumped, his heart pounding. A wizened black woman, skin like dried-up leather, sat on the porch rocker of the bait store.

"Who are you?" He croaked, his voice high.

"Folks hereabouts calls me Sweet Mary. Jackson tell me come."

"Jackson? What on earth for?"

"He say you give me a token."

"What kind of token?"

The woman rose and shuffled forward. Bugle sniffed at the air, whined, and sidled closer to Tom.

"You got a tin of buttons. You go fetch me that red flower one."

"Those were Helen's old saved buttons. She liked the colors."

"I knows that. I wait here till you gets it."

Tom frowned. Holding the screen with his foot, he fumbled with the lock. Opening the glass half-door, he stood aside while Bugle trotted past and took up his customary station near the window.

The button tin sat on the smooth wood counter. Tom scrunched his eyebrows and shook his head. *I don't remember pulling that tin down. Don't remember leaving out that other button I found either.*

Opening the box, he fingered a flower shaped button on top. *Does this feel warm or am I imagining?* He stepped back onto the porch.

The crone held out a spidery brown hand. Puzzled, he gave her the red button. She wrapped it in a crumpled, stained dollar bill, slipped the bundle in her pocket, then hobbled down the steps and disappeared among the cattails.

A blue-black crow flew across the asphalt road, perched briefly in a gnarled sycamore, then flew on.

The button and granny woman made Tom think about Bo and his years at the paper mill. The man had held the place in an iron fist. He decided hiring, firing, and assignments to the dangerous, dirty jobs—a personification of the town's faults. Tom felt queasy at the memory.

• • •

The easy routine of the sleepy fishing community helped Tom tamp down old memories and hurt. He liked talking with charter boat owners, storekeepers, and townspeople. He even knew the mailman on a first name basis, something he'd not done in Jasper.

Mail, delivered in the middle of the afternoon, gave Tom and Jackson a break in their day. They relished picking through the sale flyers, reading the weekly hometown news from Jasper, and casually jawing with each other. On light delivery days, the postman usually sat, drank a coke, and talked with them.

One early November afternoon, the mail carrier, running behind, delivered his route an hour later than usual. Tom had pulled two orange popsicles from the cooler and handed one to Jackson who sat on the porch and rested his back against a post. Both had finished their dripping treats by the time the postman arrived.

Tom took the mail and plunked down in a straight back chair. Opening the newspaper, he leaned against the wall and balanced the chair on two legs.

"Jackson, look at this." Tom dropped his chair onto four legs with a resounding thunk. "Bo Watkins died."

"That a fact? What it say?"

Tom folded the paper and read in a measured voice:

> Benjamin Charles Watkins, age 54, known to his co-workers and friends as Bo, died in his home Thursday, October 31. No cause of death was identified. For twenty years, Watkins managed the St. Regis Paper Mill. He was a member of the Jasper Rotary Club and the Conservative Businessmen of Hamilton County. Funeral arrangements are pending.

"What do you make of that?"

"I don't know, Mr. Tom, but I say let the devil hold that man close to his bosom."

A week later, Sweet Mary, appeared in the doorway.

"I brung you this here red button. I trade it back for a tobacco plug."

"I forgot you had it." Tom chuckled and extended his hand. She placed the flower-shaped plastic in his palm. "Why, it feels warm."

"I been holding it here." She patted her left shirt pocket. "Now you reach me down that Beechnut."

He hesitated a moment, pulled the tobacco off a shelf, and handed it to her. She nodded, smiled slightly, and shuffled out of the store.

Dust motes rose in dervish clouds at her passing and glinted briefly in the afternoon light. A striped cat, busy grooming his whiskers, lounged on the porch. The pungent odor of fish and salt mingled.

"I always wondered how that old hag knew about Helen's tin and her favorite button. And how it came to be sitting out." Tom watched her go.

"I set that tin out," said Jackson.

"You? How did you know about it?"

"My mama give you that tin to keep when we cleaning up. She say keep it, cause it Missus Helen's. You put that tin up on that top shelf years back when you first bought this here store. Day Bo Watkins showed up, you found a button. He missing a shirt button when he here."

"Did you tell Sweet Mary to ask for Helen's button?"

"Naw. But I give her that wet, sweaty bill Bo Watkins threw at me."

Both men stood silent, eyes locked.

"Did Mary conjure Bo Watkins?"

"I don't rightly know." Jackson rubbed his head. "Talk have it that man done choked to death on a fish bone."

Tom stared toward the swamp where Sweet Mary had disappeared. He sat on the porch and rubbed the red button between his thumb and forefinger.

A sodden breeze stirred the cattails. A crow, raucous and bragging, flapped toward a stand of pine and disappeared in the morning promise. Contentment settled across Tom's face as he watched the day begin.

The Roses Are Beautiful This Year

Carrie slid onto the piano bench, fingered the yellowed ivory keys, and began Chopin's "Opus 48." Anguished notes and broken chords hung in the air a moment and then evaporated into the corners of the music room. A sliver of sunlight trembled across the oak floor. She caressed a single, final C, stood, and strolled into the parlor toward her sister.

"Marie, dear, our agent called. She has a family to bring by next week." Carrie's no-nonsense voice underscored her angular face and gray eyes. "You know when that swamp crone pokes around, it's time for another offering."

"Yes, I know. But let's not think about that." Marie ignored what she found distasteful. Gray hair, drawn up in perky curls atop her head, gave her a youthful appearance despite her seventy-two years.

Carrie twisted her hands as if washing, her veins in blue ropes under translucent skin. "Strangers. Yankee strangers at that, they poke and gawk. The thought annoys me. "

"But the roses are beautiful this year."

"Except our Black Stephen." She stood in silhouette, her back to Marie. "He's quite stressed. He needs care."

"Oh, sister dear, don't be so negative."

"*One* of us has to manage our obligations if we are to continue living here at Meriwether." Carrie swallowed and pressed her lips into a thin line. "Maybe these Yankees will meet our *minimum prerequisites.*"

Marie adjusted her wire rimmed glasses. "How do you know they're Yankees?"

"Because our sales agent said they'll be here from Rochester, New York. I believe he works for Xerox up there." Carrie parted the tattered front drapes. "He's a corporate type and you know how opinionated they are." She released the dingy material, allowing it to fall back across the window.

Marie glanced up and nodded. "Does he have a family?"

"Yes, a wife and daughter. He left the daughter back in New York. I'm told she's in boarding school."

"Northerners still have a penchant for marching through Georgia. It irritates me. We must simply be careful to collect what we need and send them on their way."

Spinster sisters, Marie and Carrie, limped along lost between past family legends and modern circumstances. Periodically, a 'For Sale' sign sagged in the driveway before disappearing after a few months. The property sighed in relief.

• • •

Sodden air created a damp film on the little entourage's arrival. When Carrie saw the Thompsons, she glanced at Marie, who nodded an acknowledgement. *Rude of them to arrive late.* Carrie turned and followed Marie's flutter into the house.

"Sisters, this is Richard Thompson and his wife Nicole." The sales agent made a sweeping gesture toward the couple. Nicole inclined her head slightly, offered a thin smile, and twirled a platinum curl around a manicured finger.

Richard wiped sweat from his forehead. "Is this place air conditioned?" His body vibrated with impatience. "I can't tolerate heat."

"No, it is not." The agent smiled indulgently. "Built in 1824, it is labeled historical, specifically classic revival style. In Georgia, a nice tax break comes with this designation. Besides, the high ceilings and jib windows catch the breezes beautifully. Some improvements have been made, but air conditioning is impractical."

Nicole raised an eyebrow. She said nothing.

Richard snorted and slipped out of his sport jacket. The action did nothing to make it cooler or to improve his sour mood.

"I'd like to have a country place." Nicole cooed and stepped into the entry. "I'm quite tired of city traffic, noise, concrete canyons."

Richard glared at her and lit a cigarette.

"I want to get my career on track."

"What career? For Christ's sake, you mean that secretarial job?" Richard lowered his voice. "Be reasonable. Corporate wives do not have careers." Jaw clenched, he shifted the coat on his arm and loosened a striped tie.

"I was an executive assistant, not a secretary." Nicole frowned. "I'd like to consider something different. Maybe a floral shop."

Marie glanced at Carrie, nodded, and led the group into the formal dining room. She opened the cherry wood pocket doors that divided the parlor and library, releasing a pungent aroma of old leather and paper.

Carrie walked across the book-lined room and opened threadbare drapes. Dust motes, caught in sunlight, hung in dense, languid clouds. A portrait of a black-suited man glared down on the room's inhabitants. The half-filled crystal decanter atop a reading table sparkled.

After a moment, she led the way into the formal dining room adjacent to the parlor.

Nicole gasped and ran her hand across the walnut table that dominated the area. She floated toward the tall windows, stood a moment, and then stepped purposefully toward the French doors opening to the outside.

Taking a deep breath, she exhaled slowly, and drank in the gardens a-hum with birds and insects. Assorted plots clambered down a slope and shoved across narrow footpaths twining toward an oak grotto. Like colored dice flung by a giant hand, flowerbeds grew in profusion.

"What did you say? The heat feels so passionate and ripe. So *alive*." She closed her eyes. "I can hear it growing."

"It's the damn bugs you hear." Richard glanced down at his watch yet again. "Bugs and other vermin."

"Must you always be so critical? With no sense of the mystical?" A peevish note crept into Nicole's voice.

"I have to be in the city. I can't run my sales force from here. At least they have air conditioning there."

"Consider this a country home." Smiling, she stepped onto the sun-washed patio.

The agent took Richard's arm and guided him outside. "Of course, it would be perfect. You could bring business associates out for the weekend. Show them the Grand Old South. You know our Southern men have strong, cherished customs of hunting and handling guns. And, good bird dogs, especially in bird season. A country weekend with the Fulton County Bird and Gun Club could easily start from here."

Richard undid several shirt buttons. Chest hair, wet with perspiration, pushed through the gap. He narrowed his eyes at the agent.

"There's golf in Augusta, the Masters Tournament, and Calloway Gardens." The agent cocked her head at Nicole and continued.

"Interesting." Richard took a final drag on his cigarette and thumped it away. "How do old line southerners accept newcomers? Specifically newcomers from the North?"

"So long as they understand politics, remain discrete in racial matters, and blend in socially, they are accepted."

"What about the wives?" he asked.

"Women manage the household and social obligations," said the agent. "Corporate wives spend most of their time on charity benefits and community projects."

Nicole closed her eyes a moment and tamped down her irritation. "Don't they do other things? More interesting?"

"In the South, it's important to keep a nice home and yard as well as maintain social standing." The agent picked a stray hair off her sleeve.

Nicole ignored the remark, her mouth a pinched, narrow line. She flipped her hair off her neck. "I find corporate wives bored and boring."

Shifting her clipboard, the agent nodded toward the sisters. "Ladies, can you show Mrs. Thompson the gardens while Mr. Thompson and I look over the rest of the property?"

"Of course. Come with us, my dear." Carrie's voice took on a honeyed quality. She guided the clutch down rock steps toward daylilies nodding on thin green necks.

"You know that Yankee marauder William Sherman passed by here on his way into Atlanta." Marie had a way of chirping whenever she interrupted Carrie. "That horrible man had Great-grandfather White executed."

Carrie raised her voice and cocked an eyebrow toward her sister. "Reilly the overseer and two field darkies were shot because they had the unmitigated gall to defend Meriwether. In fact, they died right here where we're standing."

"His daughter, my grandmother, buried Great-granddaddy over there and planted a magnolia to mark his grave." Marie picked her way toward the giant tree. Craning her neck, she stared up into lichen-covered limbs. "It's grown huge over the years. Blossoms positively blanket it in spring and smell citrusy, rather heady."

Carrie poked her gnarled walking stick among the rotted leaves. "See this?" She tapped a hand-hewn rock. "His headstone. It's crumbled a little, but still right here."

"Oh, my." Nicole swallowed, her throat jerked with the action. "Buried here? Was that his portrait hung over the fireplace in the parlor?"

"Yes. He was a genuine patriarch and southern aristocrat. Suitors for our grandmother's hand stood in awe of him."

"Except that Shelby Roubideaux." Carrie paused, her hand rested on her small bosom. "He swept Grandmother off her feet. He came from family over near Baton Rouge. However, you cannot really trust Creole breeding or their claims to any real family lineage. After all, heat and passion seal the devil's covenant with the South."

Marie nodded and strolled toward the circular, jasmine-covered arbor.

Nicole bent and touched the decaying stone. A pungent, slightly sweet-sick odor permeated the air. She wrinkled her nose and drew back. Gauzy dragonflies floated past, green and blue dancers in a predatory drama.

"When Grandmother married, she stood in the rose garden and vowed to love Grandfather as long as they both lived." Marie, a romantic at heart, felt especially simpatico with her grandmother.

Gently, Carrie laid a hand on her sister's arm. "He would have lived more years had he been true." She turned to her guest. "You see, he got involved with those quadroons down in New Orleans. Why, he even moved his favorite to Atlanta shortly after our mother's nineteenth birthday."

"When Grandmother found out about it, she was so furious she shot Grandfather Shelby right in his treacherous heart. Killed him dead."

"Judge was such a gentleman about it though." Marie smoothed errant wisps of hair into place. "He let her bury Grandfather under the floribunda roses near the arbor where they took their vows."

"Good riddance to that philanderer." Carrie spoke sharply. "They let Grandmother live here so she could raise our mother. Extenuating circumstances, you understand."

Sparrows darted through the undergrowth. A striped cat crouched nearby, yellow eyes focused on the small birds. Carrie paused, watched their lively twitters, and then strolled further down the path.

"Folks are more appreciative of family obligations in the South," Marie's voice caught in her throat. "At least Grandmother kept her vow. She did love him as long as *both* lived."

"His mistress came here after that."

"Mistress? Here? To live?" Nicole shook her head and blinked.

"Why, yes." Marie glanced at her sister. "Remember? Grandmother hired that woman to care for mother and later us girls."

Carrie's voice was flat, expressionless. "What was that poor yellow wench to do all alone? She had always been *kept*. When she first came, her work habits were sorry. Of course, Grandmother taught her about her new duties."

"Yes, what do kept women do but shop and attend parties? And, of course, that *other obligation*." Marie fluttered her lace hankie. "Mother had her buried under the yellow roses when she died. Don't you think that poetic? And kind?"

"Three people are buried here?" Color drained from Nicole's face. "Is that common in the South? You bury people in the backyard?"

"Oh, dearie, people need to be home, with family. It's our connection with each other. I don't rightly recall exactly how many are resting here." Carrie continued toward the grotto.

"Mother is buried over there." Marie gestured to a troupe of white azaleas near several stately pines. "An ode to purity."

Tiny insects flitted through sunlit humidity. The sisters linked arms, whispered, and strolled several steps farther, heads bent toward each other.

Nicole's hand trembled. She stumbled, caught herself, and gravely concentrated on the path. Goosebumps pricked along her neck.

Readjusting her straw hat, Carrie hobbled toward a dense garden corner partially hidden by a moss-shrouded oak. Shadows striped the path.

Marie dabbed at her face, her cheeks flushed pink. "Sister dear, I must go in. I feel rather wilted in this heat."

Carrie frowned. "Do go in. I'll finish this *obligation*, this tour." She leaned on her walking stick.

Nodding weakly, Marie turned toward the house.

"My sister does not like this part of the garden, says it makes her feel faint," said Carrie. "She's not as strong as I am. Not as resolute. I care for the garden because she is so, shall we say, fragile? I enjoy keeping the old line roses alive."

"But aren't they difficult, temperamental? And they have thorns."

"Oh, of course, there are thorns, but every living thing harbors a sharp edge someplace."

Curious, Nicole followed the older woman into the grotto gloominess. Weak sunlight dappled the ground. A marble obelisk stood phallic-like in the shadows, water stains and burnt smudges marring its cracked pedestal. A single rose bush grew at the base. A stench of entities no longer alive permeated the clearing.

"This rose is such a dark crimson, it's almost black. I thought roses needed sunlight. How does this one survive?" Nicole leaned closer and curled her hands around a single blossom jutting out on a thick thorny cane.

"Move closer. Smell it." Carrie motioned with her stick.

Nicole took a deep breath, closed her eyes. Her hands coiled around the nodding bloom. "Ouch! Damn it." She jerked away. Several delicate scratches glistened on her hand. A single drop of blood trembled on a fingertip.

"My dear, you have hurt yourself. Here, let me blot it away. We don't want to spoil things with carelessness." Carrie dabbed at the fat, red glob.

"Oh, thank you." Nicole stared perplexed at her finger. "I didn't mean to do that. And, now I've ruined your beautiful lace handkerchief."

"Never mind, my dear. Here, I'll put it away." Tenderly, Carrie folded the cloth around the moist splotch and tucked it in her pocket.

"Still, it is an unusual color for a rose."

"Yes, it is. It's called Black Stephen."

"Do you name all of your roses?"

"No, of course not. Only the very *special* ones." Carrie paused, a thin smile played along her lips.

"It's for a man we both knew rather, shall we say, intimately? The rose reminds us of his heart. We buried it here."

"Another person's buried here?"

"No, not him. His heart, my dear. A swamp crone, a hag, suggested his heart and an occasional sacrifice would feed the rose and preserve the color."

Nicole's face paled. "Sacrifice? What kind of sacrifice?"

"You misunderstand. Actually, it's similar to a church when they burn incense and offer communion. A symbolic gesture to remind us of past events, simply meant to renew a vow or promise. Nothing elaborate. It's only a manner of speaking."

Carrie ran her hand along the stained marble, bent to the blossom, lips slightly parted, and inhaled deeply. The rose trembled as she exhaled. "We don't really believe in such things but the Negras hereabouts do."

The moss-draped limbs of an ancient oak groaned. A breeze stirred the gray spiral cascades.

Nicole shivered. "Who is that old woman?"

"I don't see anyone."

"Right there." She pointed toward a stone bench. "There with the striped cat."

"My dear. No one's here but us." Carrie stepped next to Nicole and placed a hand on her forearm.

Nicole's voice rose. "I saw her. She was chanting. And that cat hissed and glared with those awful eyes."

"No, you are wrong. No one is here but the two of us. Perhaps you saw the shadows shifting."

Nicole stumbled. "I'm not sure now. I feel confused."

Standing on the edge of the patio, Richard bellowed, his voice ratcheting high with impatience. "Nicole, I've got a plane to catch. Come immediately. I cannot spend all day around this crumbling relic with these women."

"Yes, Richard. Coming," Nicole stepped onto the narrow path then paused a moment. "I wish he would consider my needs more."

"Bless your heart, my dear. Men often forget to pay attention. Sometimes we have to encourage them in unusual ways." Carrie leaned toward Nicole conspiratorially. "Help them understand things from a different angle."

"What do you mean?"

"You must bargain. Southern womenfolk use whatever is at our disposal. The old darkies say our desires, our *needs*, are satisfied when sealed with blood and a burnt offering."

"What should I bargain for?"

"Whatever you desire. Power? Wealth? Love? A different life, perhaps?"

Nicole shuddered. "What a strange way to believe. Still, if I had power . . . then wealth and a different life could happen. I'll think about this."

"Yes, think about it."

In the distance, a crow cawed, loud and raucous. Rotted leaves obscured the ground and released a musk brown odor. Suspended on a thorn, a red drop quivered and turned black in the afternoon shadows.

Nicole turned and strode out of grotto dimness into the glaring heat. Following, Carrie fingered the linen stuffed in her pocket and smiled for the second time that day.

Richard waited near the patio French doors. "My god, the heat is suffocating." He lit a cigarette, sucked in a long drag, and exhaled through his nostrils. Smoke twisted up and disappeared in the sunlight.

"Richard, I want to live in the country."

"No, I think not." With an abrupt gesture, he flicked the cigarette in a bright arc into purple petunias. Turning, he strode into the house.

Nicole extended her hand to Carrie. "Thank you for showing me your gardens. Your ideas are a bit curious but, still, I enjoyed our talk."

Carrie patted the younger woman's hand. "Sister says I prattle on too much. But ritual and bargaining are a part of living."

"Yes, *quid pro quo.*" Nicole smiled, turned, and followed Richard.

The agent stuffed a sheaf of papers into her briefcase. "The heat is so heavy. You and Marie should stay in the house where it's less oppressive. I'll show the Thompsons out."

"Thank you. That's very kind of you, my dear." Carrie watched the threesome move through the music room and out the front entry.

Unable to resist, Nicole plunked a single high C as she passed the piano. The eerie note reverberated against the closing door.

"Have they gone?" Marie materialized from the library and glided through the French doors onto the patio. "Did they offer anything?"

Carrie poked among the potted flowers, retrieved the smoldering, half-smoked cigarette and laid it gently on the lace-edged linen.

"Yes. The usual."

"Freely given?"

"Of course."

She turned toward the shadow-shrouded obelisk and purposefully strode across the lawn.

"There, there Stephen. I'm coming."

A Letter from Canada

Anne Whitney Davis heard the funeral director speaking—a scratchy sound. Words with torn edges. A broken record playing over and over, hurting her ears. She stared at him.

"You'll need to select a burial outfit for your mother. Most folks like to use Sunday meeting day clothes. Something dignified."

She'd hunted around and finally settled on a red cotton dress with pleated skirt. Rummaging in the chest of drawers, she found a single strand of pearls and small button earrings. Anne felt weak choosing clothing fit for eternity.

Mother had dropped dead one day in October while shopping at Winn-Dixie. She fell against the Post Cereal display and scattered boxes of Spoon Size Shredded Wheat and Grape-Nuts across the aisle. The mess of boxes blocked the Wednesday afternoon shoppers.

While selecting the dress and accessories, Anne discovered the letter, bound with a water-green ribbon. When her hand first touched the crinkly paper, she jerked back. A faded red 1965 postmark perched on the corner.

I've seen this letter before. Thoughtfully, she picked it up and gently pulled the ribbon. Her thumbnail slipped under the envelope flap. A single sheet, discolored with age and folded in half, lay naked.

She scanned the signature: *Forever, my devotion, J.*

Her hand trembled. Who was "J"?

She refolded the letter and tucked it back into the fragile envelope. It didn't feel right, reading Mother's letter after all these years. Especially with her dead.

Strange she should remember the day the letter arrived and she had run breathless into the house. Her thoughts cycled backward.

• • •

"Mother, look, an airmail letter with a foreign stamp. Can I have it? For my collection?" Anne waved a red-and-blue edged envelope.

"Let me see." Mother had paused, wiped flour from her hands, and reached for the letter. She cradled it as she would a baby bird.

"Says Canada. That's Queen Elizabeth on the stamp." Anne pointed to the corner with a grubby finger.

Mother's eyes glazed over, tears brimming. She tucked the envelope in her apron pocket and continued kneading biscuit dough. Flour puffs hung in the kitchen air.

"Don't you want to know who it's from?"

"No, not right now. Go finish your homework before your daddy gets home."

"First read the letter." Anne twirled a black curl around her stubby finger. "Please."

Mother raised a white-coated hand, palm out. "No. It's *my* letter. I will not read it with you. You may not have the stamp or envelope." Frowning, she rolled the dough flat and began cutting biscuit rounds.

Anne blinked, her face scrunched. She stomped out of the kitchen and marched into her bedroom. "Sometimes Mother makes me so mad. No need to bite my head off either. Not often a letter comes from a foreign country." She banged the door closed and slumped down with her math assignment.

At school, Fridays were current events day and the students gave reports garnered from TV news or the local paper. Anne relished searching for articles about Vietnam, Civil Rights or the Apollo Space Program. Such times, the door to her world swung open to reveal ideas, countries, and people beyond her small town.

She wanted to tell about the letter, but since Mother had acted so snappish, she settled on reporting about the final evacuation from Vietnam. Last before lunch, Anne stood at the front of the room and wondered if she had time to finish.

"The American Embassy has decided to get out of Saigon. The U.S. military has sent lots of ships and planes to help people leave."

Several boys seated in the back snickered. One stuck his hand under his armpit and pumped out fart sounds.

"Ought to hang them Yankee commies and nigger lovers for running." A disembodied voice hooted from the back.

"They all cowards. Lily-liver-yellow-dog-chicken cowards." Another chortle of derision bounced around the classroom.

"Class, quiet please." Teacher—a tall, big-boned woman—grimaced and gestured impatiently. "Finish your report and sit down."

Anne shifted her note cards and glared at the boys. The bell clanged before she could continue and the general rush out of the classroom ensued.

After school, Anne trotted straight home, slammed her books down on the kitchen table, and marched into the utility room.

"How was school today?" Mother bent down and pulled towels from the dryer.

"Remember that news on TV about the evacuation?"

"Yes. Why?"

"I was giving my report when the bell rang. Billy Johnson and Henry Junior pushed me against the blackboard and ran. When I got outside on the playground, they threw rocks at me and tripped me into a mud puddle. Henry's little brother ran up behind and pinched my arm. It's already blue."

Mother turned, hands full, and stared at Anne with raised eyebrows. "Goodness gracious, you look a mess. Are you hurt?"

"I skint my hands and knee. See." Anne pointed to a seeping scrape. "And my dress got torn." Anne pointed at her ripped waistband.

"Why do you think they did that?" Mother examined the wound. "Let's put some iodine on."

"Those boys said communists like me caused us to leave Vietnam. They said *you* had black friends. That we were Negro lovers. Only they used that *other* word. They said guys that burned draft cards and ran off to Canada were faggots and cowards."

Mother paused. She stood in front of the open window. The whir of a lawn mower and snatches of conversation drifted in as neighbors settled into late afternoon routines.

When she turned from the window, she put one hand on Anne's shoulder, the other under her chin and tilted her face up.

"That war's eating our young men up. Some of them are going to Canada. Voting rights and integration are mixed into this and that scares people. Makes them do things they would not consider under different circumstances." She sighed and shook her head.

"But why? How come people call us names?"

"I'm not sure I can explain that." Mother continued folding towels, her face pensive. "You see, while I was in college, a mixed group of us lived together in a huge two-story house. No hot water and the plumbing constantly busted."

"Why did you live there?"

"Cheap rent. In an odd sort of way, it was an enriching time." She smiled, a wistful look played across her face. "We cooked, argued, laughed and studied together. We went to political rallies and demonstrated with other students. I met a young man from Mississippi at one meeting. He was sensitive. Bright."

Anne reached for a towel and began helping her mother fold.

"We got to know each other and grew close. When the march on Washington happened, he felt duty-bound to help."

"What did he do?"

"He dropped out of classes and joined the organizing groups. Became an activist."

"Did you go with him?"

"I stayed at the university. He said he'd come back but he never did."

"What happened?"

"He got in touch several times, but not regular. I knew he was involved with the Selma marches. A friend told me later that they both got draft notices and decided to move to Canada."

"Was your letter from that man?"

"Not directly. But sort of."

"What does it talk about?"

"Personal things. Ideas. Decisions. Plans." Gently, she kissed Anne's forehead and hugged her close. "It's all very complicated. I think you'll understand when you're older."

"You always say that when you don't want to explain things."

She stroked Anne's tan face and smiled.

"Did Daddy know him?"

"Yes. He did." She stared at Anne. "We were all very close. It was a different time with exceptional men and women." She stopped, turned away, and picked up the bundle of folded towels. "Your daddy will be home from work soon. Go wash up and come help me in the kitchen."

• • •

The summer before she left for the university, Anne glanced up from her packing and watched a grey Buick turn into the driveway. A man in a blue suit emerged. Her mother opened the door to his knock, stepped outside, and stood under the oak shade tree talking. Anne busied herself with selecting books and trying on clothes.

By the time she finished her packing, the man had gone. Anne yawned, stretched, and meandered into the kitchen.

She sniffed the air. "Sweet potatoes. My favorite. I love smelling brown sugar and cinnamon. Who stopped by?"

"Oh, someone I knew years ago."

"What did he want?"

"He invited me to a lecture." Mother cleared her throat, turned to the oven, and dialed the heat down.

"What about?"

"A posthumous honor for a special friend, an activist we both knew." Her voice rattled. "It's in Hattiesburg Saturday night."

Anne frowned.

"He worked with many things. Boys burning their draft cards. Moving to Canada. Amnesty. Integration. Voting. It's all rather tightly woven together."

"What was his name?"

Mother did not answer but instead pulled the yams out of the oven and placed them on a cooling rack.

Anne shrugged and turned to wash her hands. Finished, water dripping from her fingertips, she reached for the kitchen towel.

"Is this the friend that wrote you that letter?" She stared at Mother. "You know, when I was in the seventh grade? The one that helped with the Washington march? And Selma?"

"Can you please watch that pound cake? Don't let it burn." Mother nodded toward the oven.

"Yes, but you didn't answer me."

"Don't stand there dribbling water on the floor." Mother carefully took off her apron. "I think I'll be driving up to Hattiesburg Saturday."

Eyes wide and mouth open, Anne stared. "What will Daddy say?"

"We all worked together. Our relationship was different. Extraordinary." She folded her apron lengthwise, and flopped it on a chair back.

"Do you want me to go with you?" Anne touched her mother's arm.

"No. I'll do this alone."

"What about Daddy? Should he go?"

"I'd rather he not. He'll understand." She took a slow, ragged breath. "I'm going for a walk. Down to the park. Watch the cake. You and Dad eat dinner if I'm not back in an hour."

•••

The day of Mother's funeral dawned hot. Not an Indian summer hot but an I-can't-even-breathe July hot. The last handshake completed and I'm-so-sorry said, Anne and her father sat on the front church pew silent, each lost in thought. She held his work-rough hand and studied his face. He cried in coughing sobs, shaking. His shoulders drooped.

"Your mother was very independent. Strong willed. Some folks called her hard-headed. That's what I loved most. That independence. Acceptance of all sorts of people. All colors. She had ideas I never could understand," he said, his voice unsteady.

Pausing, he pulled a handkerchief out, blew his nose, and swallowed hard. "In the end, it was those things I loved most that eroded us both."

Anne wiped her swollen eyes and dabbed her nose, so raw she could barely tolerate a touch. Light spots behind her eyes signaled the insidious creep of a migraine. Her stomach knotted. Everything hurt. Emptiness settled.

"I only wanted to live here and work at the bank, build our community. She wanted a wider world, not so mundane. We talked about separating. But you needed a stable home. In the end, we stayed true to our marriage vows. In many ways, you are like her." He held Anne's hand.

"I know your mother never explained to you or anyone else why some things happened. You see, there was another man before me. He went to Birmingham then Washington and Selma. Got caught up in all that. Later we heard he decided to leave. During those years Canada was a haven for all those boys—black and white—to be safe."

Anne shook her head, her eyes riveted on his drawn face.

"She didn't talk much after he left. We married. You came along pretty quick. Some things even she wouldn't face."

Anne's hand flew to her mouth. "Oh Daddy, what are you telling me?"

He watched her dark eyes widen. Leaning, he kissed her softly on the forehead. She felt his chapped lips, rough and gentle, caress her.

"Far as I know, she only got two letters from him." He continued in a low voice. "We both heard about him but not from him. She wrote and told him about you. I don't really know if he tried to stay in touch or not."

Anne caught her breathe with an audible suck. She felt light-headed, confused. She stared at her father, frowned and heard her voice rising. "Mother did that? She never told me anything."

"Your mother was a good woman. We didn't always agree, but I did love her. Don't think she loved me back. At least, not the same. Her heart was in another place." He wobbled to standing, leaning heavy on his cane. "No matter. I have been grateful for our 42 years together. Good years. And I have loved you from the moment you came into this world."

He shuffled out into the sunshine. Anne rose and followed.

A striped cat sauntered across the street. The corner traffic light flashed from red to green. Cars stopped or accelerated with the change, creating a jumble of traffic noises. They stood a long minute and watched their community flowing pass.

"Daddy, I have to see Mother one last time."

"You go on. I'll wait here."

She leaned over and kissed his cheek.

"I love you Daddy. I love you both." Turning, she walked back into the church.

Alone, she stood next to the coffin and tenderly touched the silent face. *Good thing I chose the red dress. You always said red was strong and bold—your color.*

She pulled the letter, tied with a water-green ribbon, out of her pocket and held it like a baby bird.

"I'm still not sure I understand everything. I know you and Daddy loved me. You gave me roots. For that, I love you both."

She tucked the letter under her mother's motionless hand, smiled, turned back toward the open door, and strode into the sunlight.

Dear Sis,

Remember T-Bone Baggins? He graduated art school with me. They found his catboat out in Galveston Bay late July. No sign of him. He left that rusted Chevy pickup on the dock, keys in the ignition, his stray dog tied to the door handle. Just disappeared. No tidy conclusion for him, he's forever a mystery. I've heard drunks are like that. Good thing you didn't marry him.

Damn, but he was a handsome son-of-a-bitch.

Did I ever tell you we were lovers?

Luv, Angie

Three Friends, Class of 1970

Clint, Jake, and Roy stayed friends through grade school. Like young foxes, they tramped the woods and nosed through wild undergrowth together. They fished, skipped classes, skinny dipped, and stole cigarettes.

In high school, Jake's dad gave him an old clunker Chevy pickup. The three pooled money and bought enough gas to keep it rattling down the back roads. They drank beer and gigged frogs or hunted possum.

When the male itch grew strong, they'd pile in that truck with dates and head to the drive-in where they groped and kissed those gals until the place shut down.

Later, with the girls safely home, they'd sit at the all-night Shell Truck Stop on U.S. 90, talking. About two o'clock, scheduled for the early shift at the wheel plant, they'd leave.

Everything changed that third year out of high school.

Clint, with his devil-may-care smile, blown into meaty red pieces in Vietnam. Army sent his belongings and a folded flag back with thanks from a grateful nation. A photo of him, arms flung around his mud-splattered buddies near Hoa Phu, sits on the family mantle.

A train whacked Jake at the crossing near Siloam Mounds. Engineer didn't see that rusty truck until he'd knocked it a quarter mile down the track. Jake's wife got insurance money for what was left of the vehicle. Their son carries the same brooding good looks as his dad.

Roy married his high school sweetheart, had two girls, and worked for the highway department. His acne-scarred face turned redder each year as he sank deeper into a perpetual whiskey haze. His daughters grew up, married and moved north. With no further reason to stay, his wife left.

Alone, in the Winn-Dixie parking lot, after a high school reunion, he curled around a bottle and drowned in Kentucky brown water.

Friends, class of 1970.

The Reading, Saint Martin Parish

The applause gave Mark a feeling of euphoria and confidence. He acknowledged the group of listeners and inwardly delighted in his ability to string words together.

A New Yorker, East Village specifically, he had felt stomach-twisting apprehension at the thought of a book tour through the South. Especially a poetry book. At 38, worn with marketing hype yet struggling to build his portfolio, he consented. His editor cobbled together a Chattanooga-Birmingham-Jackson-Baton Rouge tour and added any medium-sized town in between with a bookstore and accommodating date. Mark felt like a whore.

He flew south, rented a car and meandered through the kudzu-covered humid landscape. Now, the last stop, smug at negotiating the cultural divide, he relaxed and offered a silent thank you to off-the-beaten-path independent bookstore owners that knew their clientele so well. Plenty of *us* in the South.

"I can take a few questions now." Mark nodded toward a blonde with a tri-Delt pin, her arm shyly held in the air.

"I think your poetry is absolutely divine. You speak with such authority on relationships and how they begin and end. Where do you get your ideas?

"Everywhere." He made an expansive gesture, aware of his chest hair brazenly sticking out of his slightly open shirt. "I can walk the streets of the Bronx, Chicago, Brick Town, the subway, Berkeley—really, any place—and find subjects. Snippets in the newspaper, you know those blurbs that give two sentences without really telling you anything." He stepped away from the podium and half-sat on the book table.

He flashed a smile, showing teeth his mother had insisted the dentist straighten when Mark was twelve. Embarrassed with his skinny stature and a mouth full of wire, he had spent those grade school years hiding at the back of the room.

"Question from the lady in the back row?"

The moderator hurried over and thrust the mike toward a rotund woman, her grey hair flying in abandon. She spoke with a lilting Cajun accent. "My question has to do with whether your poems come from your life or did you raid another person's experience?"

"I think every writer holds a mirror to the reader and asks 'what do you see?' It's a first criterion for writing, his stock-in-trade. If the poet is not honest with feelings, what does the reader have to gain?" Mark nodded for the next question.

Questions continued—the same in every city, every night, every bookstore.

On the fourth row, left aisle, a buff man with military style haircut leaned toward the speaker, twitching. His chair creaked.

Ever conscious of his audience, Mark locked eyes with him, half-shifted, and then continued answering questions. Self-conscious at his nervous underarm sweat, he casually rolled his sleeves up, a footnote to his khakis-and-white-shirt writerly style.

When Mark announced the final question, Military gestured for the mike. The facilitator failed to notice and instead handed off to a female student, ears rimmed with rings and her brown hair a rat's nest of curls.

The crowd buzzed and broke up. Some meandered out, a few moved toward the front table, intent on buying a slim volume and requesting a signature.

Military rose and leaned hip-cocked against the stair railing, black tee taut against biceps and flat stomach. Hunting-cat eyes fixed on Mark, he sauntered toward the book table. The book stack dwindled and fans thinned. He stopped, a few steps separating them, and feigned noncha-lance, waiting on the last person to finish her transaction.

Mark glanced toward the jeans-clad figure, quivered inwardly, and spent extra time chatting with a dumpling-shaped housewife, her face lined with wrinkles.

Finally clear of fans, Mark turned and shifted toward Military's extended hand. They shook. He noticed the cal-luses and short nails.

"My name's Alan. Enjoyed your poetry, man. Raw. Mus-cular." His voice had a slick bass quality.

They continued the handshake.

"Thank you. Always nice to see a man at a poetry read-ing." Mark allowed a note of suggestion to creep into his voice. "Do you write?"

"A few things, mostly stuff from Afghanistan. The usual. Life at a COP, buddy issues, boredom, death."

"COP?"

"Combat outpost. Maybe you'd like to see some of my work?"

Mark picked up a pen from the table and stroked it. "I try not to raise expectations by reading my fans' poems."

"That's probably wise. But, after a tour in the Kush, you realize everything's a dice roll. Like trying to hold moon dust. I've got no expectations." He glanced down and fingered a book. "You hanging in town overnight?"

"Well, yes."

"I've got a box of Chablis in the fridge. Cheddar cheese wedge, Triscuits. We can work on those while you look over my poems. What do you say?" He stared directly into Mark's eyes.

Mark leaned back against the podium. It rocked slightly. Thoughts of yet another evening in a standard vanilla hotel and ubiquitous restaurant offering cardboard food loomed. Boxed wine and crackers weren't exactly gourmet, but the company might work.

At the front, the bookstore cash register hummed as late customers paid for lattes and house coffee. A few stragglers browsed the sale table. A store helper boxed the sound equipment and stacked chairs, creating a steady bustle and clink of sound. Outside, drizzle coated the brick street in a pale wet film. Different towns and other nights softly muttered his name. Bored, his muse screamed.

The shop door banged open in a gust of wind. The dumpling housewife flew through. No umbrella, her hair hung in damp strings. She scurried to his table breathless.

"Sorry to interrupt but I forgot to have you sign my book." Pushing in front of Military, she fumbled to the title page. "I meant to have you sign earlier but we were talking and I got distracted." She blushed. Her hand fluttered to her throat. The book flopped closed.

Mark took a pen from the table, smiled at her, and re-opened the volume. He signed his name with fashionable loops, underlining it with a flourish. "No bother. We were finished."

Muttering a thank you, she tucked the book in a pocket and turned away.

Another one-night stand, a gross deception played out as a new relationship, made him ache. Especially at the end of this tour. In the South.

He stepped behind the table and collected the remaining books. Glancing at the sinewy figure before him, he shrugged.

The moment broken, Military nodded. "I hear you, bro." He arched an eyebrow and turned away, striding through the biographies and past the gardening display. The 'Closed' sign swung lightly against the door. A pelting rain replaced the drizzle.

The Cornbread War

The Wilkerson sisters, Irene and Eunice, arrived together for the October Pot Lunch and Bingo Night. The Mount Judea Baptist Church considered bingo, even as a source of funds, gambling and therefore forbidden. The Shiloh Methodist Church parishioners commented that one dollar for a card and a handful of tokens to cover called numbers could hardly be denounced as sinful.

An early autumn coolness hung in the air, so naturally everyone brought a dish to ward off any winter doldrums. That bald fool, bachelor Pete Wilson, stood at the church community room door and leered at all the women, married or not, young or old. He claimed to have eclectic tastes.

"Why, look here. Both you beautiful ladies brought cornbread again tonight." Pete opened the door with a grand sweep of his arm for the sisters, bowed slightly, and sniffed the air.

"I love cornbread. No one has ever been able to make cornbread like my dear departed Mama." He cocked an eyebrow. "Why I think I'll marry any woman that can cook like her." He winked at Eunice, half turned, and aimed a sly grin at Irene.

"Do get out of the way, Pete." Irene balanced one pan on top the other. "I'll end up splashing this mess of turnip greens all over the place if you keep piddling around and blocking the door."

A tall, plain spinster, Irene exuded a no nonsense demeanor. Her hair, once raven black, had salted into a dingy grey. She limped from an old accident at the swimming hole when she jumped off the rope swing while a teenager.

"While you two are jawing, I might drop my pots." Eunice, as round as her sister was angular, had tiny feet and giggled at male attention. She minced into the church meeting hall behind her sister and waddled toward tables groaning under casseroles, whole hams, deviled eggs, and baked sweet potatoes. A gossamer film of odors hung almost visible in the stuffy community hall. Folding metal chairs lined the walls. Eunice set her beans and cornbread down on the near corner, carefully placing them first in the serving line and smirked at Irene, who moved pots and dishes around to make room for her greens and cornbread.

At precisely 6:30, Preacher Thompson stepped into the middle of the room, raised his arms, and announced, "Let us pray." Dutifully, chatter slacked off.

"Lord, bless this gathering of souls and the food we consume in behalf of your work. Give us strength. Amen." Usually hungry, Preacher Thompson offered short blessings for most Wednesday bingo sessions.

The last syllable uttered, Irene grabbed a plate and hustled about fixing Pete a plate of collards and cornbread.

"Any *real cook* simply cannot put sugar in cornbread no matter what." She muttered as she busied herself with Pete's plate. "Bacon fat, stone ground yellow meal and a little salt. Best to use buttermilk if you have it on hand.

That's cornbread, pure and simple. Pour that into a hot iron skillet and pop it in the oven." She sashayed over to Pete.

Eunice, scant seconds ahead, handed him a bowl of her beans with a cornbread slice. She sat with ample hips pressed discretely against his chicken-skinny legs. Not one to wait, Pete shoved beans into his mouth, dentures snapping, and sopped at the plate.

With one hand, Irene deftly grabbed the beans from Pete and with the other slipped her buttered cornbread and pepper-sauce-laced greens into his hands.

"Lordy, lordy, will you look at this. Cornbread and pot likker." Pete's voice dripped satisfaction and a grin spread across his face. "You two the best cooks in all of north Georgia. Why I'd marry one of you if I could ever figure who makes the best cornbread."

Eunice jumped up, her chair scraping on the linoleum floor. She snatched the plate of greens away, shoved her beans into Pete's hands again and glared toward Irene.

"You have the most tasteless cornbread in the whole county. It's like eating yellow cardboard."

"Sister *dearest*, he hasn't finished with the plate I just gave him," said Irene. "For your information, he doesn't need to eat that sugary stuff you make. He can get pie if he wants something sweet."

"Ladies, ladies let's not get into a fray over this." Preacher hustled across the community room, exasperation crept into his voice. "Let's eat and enjoy our bingo. Just this *one* night. Please. No squabbles." He held his arms out and began to shepherd the sisters away from Pete. The two women inched along under Preacher's gentle prodding toward the opposite side of the room.

Wiping his mouth on his shirtsleeve, Pete ambled to the laden table for seconds and heaped it full of widow Maude Smith's tuna-and-cheese casserole.

"I can't let a week go by without tuna casserole." He glanced up at Maude. "Your casserole is the best. Rivals my mother's. Is that tarragon I taste?"

She pursed her lips into an "O" and sidled along the opposite side of the serving table, keeping step with Pete, hand fluttering at her neck.

Having settled the Wilkerson sisters, one on either side of a small gas heater near the bingo decorations, Preacher returned to his own heaping plate, now cold. Raised to not waste food, he ate most of it, got a clean plate, and sliced himself a thick chunk of German chocolate cake.

Just as Preacher filled his second cup of coffee, a fistful of chips careened off his head. Startled, he dropped the steaming coffee, watched the cup bounce off the table edge, and gasped as it splashed across his lap and down his legs.

"Jesus in a raincoat chasing Judas. Those old biddies and that reprobate are running randy." Thankfully, he muttered under his breath and the blasphemy went unnoticed.

"You are a vile, selfish heifer and not fit to be a Wilkerson." Eunice stood between the bingo caller's stand and zinnia flower arrangement, her peach complexion glowing.

"Watch who you call names. Mama favored you and God may love you but I don't. You are a born hussy chasing after anything in pants." Irene sent Eunice one of her killing looks.

Grabbing another handful of tokens, Eunice stepped toward Irene and gave her a quick shove. Irene stumbled backwards several steps, caught herself, and glared at her sister.

Folks stopped mid-bite and turned. Several women hurried to the serving table intent on saving anything breakable. One boy grabbed half a pecan pie, stood near the doorway, and ate straight from the pan.

"Don't be such a rock-headed ninny about your cornbread. You only started using sugar right after Daddy died." Irene's voice rose an octave.

"Well, you baked that tasteless stuff because you thought Daddy wanted it." Eunice thrust her chin forward and scowled.

"Mama was dead and gone within six months after Daddy. She never even *asked* for any more cornbread. She preferred hot biscuits and butter."

"You might've been Daddy's favorite but Mama loved me the best."

"That's because I was like Daddy—practical. We both had our feet on the ground." Irene smirked and flounced across the room.

Eunice flung tokens in a rainbow arc over Irene. They scattered across the floor in willy-nilly directions. Several, stuck under the piano foot pedals, remained undiscovered until a week later during Sunday Bible class.

Grimacing, Preacher scuttled toward the two women, arms outstretched, coffee spill dark across his pants.

"Ladies! Ladies! Please. Let's remember where we are and who we are."

"I know who I am and I know who that man chaser is." Irene pointed. "I hate to admit she's my sister but I promised Mama I'd look after her."

"I don't need you to look after me. I need you to stay out of my business."

Pete Wilson edged over to the primary school teacher. "I can tell from all the cinnamon that you baked this apple pie.

Why, it is almost as good as my mother made." He wiped his mouth with a paper napkin, smiled, and turned back to watch the fray.

Irene's hair tumbled loose from her bun and stuck out in wild corkscrew spirals.

Eunice shoved Irene, who stumbled against the dessert table. A bowl of lime Jell-O and two dishes of banana pudding tottered for a moment then tipped over, colors puddling on the floor.

Preacher rolled his eyes and shook his head. "Ladies, this is most undignified. We cannot tolerate this behavior. Again."

"I'm not going to fight you any longer for Pete Wilson. He's got liver spots all over his bald head and false-teeth breath. You can have him and good riddance." Eunice sniffed and crossed her arms over her ample bosom.

"I don't want that old degenerate." Glaring, Irene stood, hands on her sharp hips and assumed a saintly superiority.

Town tongues wagged even before the sisters left and bingo ended. Baptists laid the wild behavior off on Methodist backsliding and the evils of gambling. Methodists responded that Pete Wilson was a Mount Judea Baptist visitor at Shiloh Church and should have minded his manners. Folks denounced the whole incident as unbecoming for churchwomen close to seventy-five.

Afterwards, clockwork regular, the sisters showed up once a month for bingo and potluck. Grande dames, they marched into the church hall side-by-side refusing to bring another covered dish, and certainly not any cornbread.

Folks ignored Pete Wilson and, thank goodness, he took the hint and stayed over at the Baptist Church.

But, truth be told, from that night on, everyone missed the drama.

Postcard: Fort Worth Stockyards, Texas

Dear Sis,

Can you believe this? Twice a day, drovers on real live cow horses herd Texas longhorns down Exchange Avenue in the Fort Worth stockyards, got on cowboy gear and all. Like the old west except for tourists gawking and the cars. Cattlemen's Steak House serves up calf fries (testicles to you greenhorns) and grilled T-bones. I've almost run out of money. Judging from the size of my head this morning, it's certain the White Elephant Saloon does NOT water down their drinks.

Will be home late Monday.

Luv, Angie

The Trickster

At forty plus, with a couple of hard marriages behind her, Maude found herself catering most often to her steady, known customers. Tonight she sat at the back of the poolroom and watched the tourists and conventioneers drift through the pseudo movie-style saloon, looking for the Old West as it never existed. Real working cowhands and homeboys generally favored Clem's Pool Hall further down the street next to the Cowtown Café.

The man caught her eye when he limped in and sat alone at the bar. His great white hair and faded eyes gave him an aura of high lonesome. He smelled of livestock, a rich earthy fragrance. She figured him for a local, down on his luck.

She watched him awhile, rose, and edged her way down the bar, elbowing a younger woman aside, stepping on the blonde's foot as she pushed past.

"Oops. Sorry, honey but this is my gig. Besides, sweetie, he's too old and not your style." She threw a harsh smile at the woman, sidled forward and brushed her hips across the man's backside. She sat on the stool next to him.

"What do you say we get out of here and get a cup of coffee?" She had a rich, slow twang and a mellow voice that belied her years in smoke-filled rooms. The accent, coupled with a few built-in extra pounds of coziness, made her unique.

"I came in to watch the crowd and have a beer. Listen to the band. No offense but I'm okay where I am." He did not turn nor look at her.

"Maybe you heard they have colder beer here. Or a better crowd." She clicked her nails on the bar and signaled the barkeep for a beer. "You know what? I think maybe you need to be around people. Female people, to be exact."

"Could be. Could be I want to mind my own business." His face had the stamp wind and sun grinds into a person who makes a living outside. He toyed with his glass and gazed at the amber liquid pooled in the bottom.

She leaned close to his shoulder and smiled playfully. "Most folks like you are down at Cowtown or Clem's."

"That so? Now what kind am I?" His voice had a stale-smoke quality. He leaned back and gave her an appraising look.

"Well, you might be local. Maybe a rancher or cowhand out of luck. Or, you could be a millionaire out slumming." She sipped her drink, brown eyes shining as she teased.

The man nodded. He fumbled in his shirt pocket, pulled out a cigarette and held it unlit between his teeth. "Could be. Then again, maybe not."

She glanced at his callused hands and knotted finger joints.

He lit his smoke and glanced at her, taking in her grey-streaked auburn hair, muted by the barroom lights. "Could be I came to hear the music. Could be I'm mixed up and lost."

They drank in silence while he smoked. Finished, he crushed the butt out, nodded, and swung off the barstool.

"Sure, lady, let's get out of here." He threw a few bills on the bar, took her elbow, and guided her toward the door. He paused outside on the plank sidewalk and lit another cigarette.

Even at night, Fort Worth felt hot and sticky, a result of the late spring rains. Tourists sweated through their new cowboy duds as they cruised the bars looking for cold beer, the mythic West, and Texas souvenirs. Maude and the man walked toward the Stockmen's Hotel, weaving around drunks, locals, and out-of-towners.

Long past its prime, the hotel rented rooms by the hour or the night. Maude's local traffic usually drifted that way while the tourist crowd and conventioneers preferred the Hilton at Sundance Square. The rodeo boys used the cheaper Motel 6 out on the bypass, mostly with their buckle bunnies, while a few old ropers riding the circuit still looked her up when in town.

A low, grey form trotted across the alley next to the hotel, paused, glared in their direction, and vanished as quickly as it had appeared.

"I'll be damned. A coyote." She stopped mid-stride and looked in the direction the wild thing had disappeared. "I like those song dogs. They are smart and resourceful. They survive, no matter what."

"Was a time I'd a-shot him." The man flipped his spent smoke aside. "But, if they can live in these damn towns with tourists and cowboy wanna-bes swarming ever' where, then more power to them." With a sun-browned hand, he pushed his weathered hat further back. "Some say they kill newborn calves. Some say they only get the weak ones would've died anyway."

"And what do you say?"

"I've knowed them to get in and out of a chicken yard without a squawk while you're inside eating breakfast. I've seen them spot a trap, toss a stick at it, and spring the dern thing. Mostly they keep field mice down and eat little stuff. They sure 'nuf survivors." He continued walking. "How is it you know about coyotes?"

She smiled. "Oh, I lived in south Texas along the border growing up. We never had our own place. Always had to lease. I've heard tell the Navajo call coyotes creators, shape shifters and tricksters. Sometime they play the fool but they always endure. Enduring. Guess that's the whole story, isn't it?"

"Maybe. Now, me, I think it's the shape shifting. Every critter's got to change with the times. Adapt. Shift."

They turned into the Stockmen's. Frayed chairs and threadbare carpets scattered around the lobby reflected some past grandeur. Strategically placed spittoons testified to an era of well-heeled ranchers and cattle money. A dust encrusted Texas longhorn head hung above the defunct fireplace.

Maude stepped to the front counter. "Enrique, give us room 216, down at the end." She held out a manicured hand for the key. "You ever wash that greasy hair? Maybe dry off that wet back?" She cocked her head and smiled, fingers tapping on the mahogany desk.

"Si. Whenever you gringos quit whining about the Alamo." The man bantered back, handed her an old-fashioned key.

She led the way up the creaking steps toward a corner room, unlocked an antique door, and flicked on table lamps. A window on either side offered views of the auction pens, rail yards and gin mills that lined the street. Although individual bathrooms had been added, the rooms still sported pitchers set on old-fashioned washbasins. Gauzy curtains covered the windows flanked by heavy maroon drapes. She liked the incongruent mixture of faded glory and modern convenience.

"How you want to handle this?" she asked. "I don't do bareback and I don't do Greek."

"I ain't a-want to handle anything right now. You go get a bottle of Jack from down at the bar and come back." The man took his hat off, tossed it on the bed, and handed her a twenty before dragging a straight-back chair over to the window. He sat heavily, put one booted foot on the sill and leaned back.

Maude stood for a moment. Her older customers often felt more relaxed if they could talk awhile. She shrugged and went out the door.

• • •

"Enrique, you know the feller that came in with me?"

"Don't really know him . . . know about him. Name's Harlan Smith. He used to own a ranch over near Abilene some time back. Had bad luck, roamed around some, then ended up here."

"Yeah? Like what kind of bad luck?"

"Well, as I recall hearing, his only boy got killed in the '68 Tet offensive. About that time, his wife took cancer. As soon as the son's body got shipped home, she gave up and died."

Maude hesitated, and then clicked across the floor and through the swinging doors into the hotel bar for a bottle.

As she walked back past the desk, she paused. "What else you know about him?"

"Nothing much. He quit windmill riding a few years back and rented the old McCall place on the south side of town. Neighborhood keeps crowding in on the house and barn. He lives alone, keeps some stray mutt, and two broke-down horses. Works a few odd jobs around. Comes in and hangs out around the Café and Clem's occasionally. Mostly stays to himself."

"Thanks."

She climbed the steps and re-entered the room. The man had opened a window. She poured two drinks, sat the bottle down, and pulled up a chair. Street sounds, like water over stones, flowed through. The noises did not disturb them. They sipped their whiskey without talking for the better part of an hour.

"You know, I been alone since my wife died in '69." Maude heard regret resonate in his voice.

"That's a long time." She reflected on her own misspent decisions and lost loves. Mother dead of cancer when she was in grade school. Mostly raised by her grandmother on a weedy place out from town. Four brothers who scattered as soon as they graduated. Father working oil field jobs to keep them afloat. She married at nineteen, went through three marriages in eight years. *God knows I've traveled a hard enough road.*

Minutes eked past slowly before he spoke again. "Yeah. A long time. My boy first and then she went. The two girls left."

"You miss them?"

"The wife sometimes. Maybe the boy."

"After I left home, I went to Beaumont, worked there awhile, moved to San Antone, and finally on up here. Fort Worth's nice enough, even with the outsiders crowding in and the tourists running amuck."

They talked, watched the street and felt the breeze slip through the room.

About two, he stood, stretched, pulled out a wad of bills and placed them on the dresser. "For your time."

He picked up his hat and started out, then stopped and scratched an address on the empty liquor bag. He laid it carefully next to the bills.

"I got a rent house on the south side. I want you to come down there next day or two."

Maude looked him in the eye. "I don't go to a john's house. Never know what you might step into."

"That so? Well, you come on down some afternoon. Got something I'll show you." Harlan walked out, his footsteps thumping down the hall.

She picked up the bills and, as an afterthought, tore the address off the sack, and stuffed it into her pocket.

Dawn gently pushed night aside by the time she walked back toward her car. She reached for the door handle, then noticed two half-grown coyotes at a restaurant dumpster, arguing over the remains of someone's meal. She watched until they looked up and silently melted into the pink morning half-light.

• • •

With the Shriners Convention in town and the summer tourist traffic at Billy Bob's, two months drifted by before Maude thought about Harlan Smith. One slow, hot Sunday afternoon, between things, she reconsidered. *What the hell? Might as well drive down to the south side and look the old man up. He said he lived where the barrio met the country, kind of a no man's border between town trash and ranch land.*

• • •

She pulled into a gravel driveway and parked beside a battered pickup. A scruffy dog lay on the porch. He lifted his whiskery head but did not bark.

She stood for a minute by her car, uncertain, fingered her car keys, and then hollered. "Hello the house. Anybody home?"

There was no answer. She pulled out the torn paper and rechecked the address.

White paint peeled off the wood siding and the porch steps knelt in the dirt. Scraps of trash, caught in the fence, fluttered like trapped birds. She stepped around the house far enough to see a dilapidated barn and corral. As she walked toward the buildings, the dog rose stiff-legged and followed. She picked her way through the weeds, looking down.

"I'd done give up on you getting by." Her head snapped up at his raspy voice.

"Well, I've been pretty busy. Just now had a chance to break loose." She continued walking. The mutt trotted ahead toward the man, tail wagging.

"Glad you came."

"Yeah? Why's that?"

"No particular reason. Dog didn't even bark at you. Must figure you're okay."

"You said you wanted to show me something."

"I really want to give you a ride."

Maude paused and cocked an eyebrow at him. "That so?"

He gestured toward two horses tied at the barn. "I was just brushing them. Sorta planning on saddling up. What did you think I meant?"

"Riding?" She smiled. "Now I haven't thrown a leg over a horse since I was a girl in Laredo. My dad worked on a spread before he wore out and left Mom. Don't know how good I'll be."

"You don't forget." He gestured toward a tack room. "Grab that saddle and cinch old Chief up."

The sorrel, spavined and grayed around the muzzle, looked half asleep. She shoved her car keys in her jeans and saddled the gelding.

• • •

The riders twisted and turned through alleyways, down a gravel road, across several empty lots and between junk-piled yards, always skirting the main roads.

Finally, Harlan reined his paint mare to a stop at the edge of a muddy dribble. He sat easy, like a person that had spent a lifetime on a horse. She relaxed back in her saddle and loosened the reins for Chief to nibble dried grass. It felt good to be out and on a horse again.

"Isn't this near Clear Fork? Part of the Trinity River?"

"Yep. Town's caught up with it though. At least the poor side has." He lit a smoke, threw one leg around the saddle horn and relaxed into the past.

"I rode windmills in West Texas. Being alone, check-ing the tanks and mills, suited me. I could ride for hours and not cross a road or see a building. Always had a dog, but he died. This yellow cur took up with me about five months ago."

He finished the cigarette, dropped his boot into the stirrup and nudged the horse down a bank. Maude pressed the sorrel forward. They crossed a dry wash and picked up a slow lope along a barbwire-flanked dirt road. A half mile further, Harlan pulled the paint to a walk and angled toward the fence line.

"You see that little mound?" He pointed to a hole almost hidden by bunch grass.

"Yeah. I see it. A den of some kind. Maybe a coyote?"

"I been watching that female for a coupla years now. Her 'n' those pups mostly eat mice, bird eggs and such as that along the fencerows. When winter comes and they get older, she'll teach them to scavenge town garbage." He stopped and propped his hands on the saddle, sat looking at the field.

A dry wind stroked the grass and sang toward open land. A late model pickup dusted past, music blaring. The driver did not appear to notice the two riders. Dust boiled up, and then settled, tinting the roadside a soft ash grey.

"We killed off the buffalo and the wolf. But coyotes have prospered. Like that one using this here pasture so close in. She's learned to shift, change with the times. A survivor." He reined his mare around and started a slow walk back toward town. "Those coyotes are clever. Otie. That's what we called them back then. Otie."

Maude let the gelding amble alongside. She listened, sensing his need to ramble through old thoughts.

"After my boy got killed and the wife died, I sold out. Couldn't make it alone on that place. Too full of memories."

"What about your girls? Didn't they want to ranch?"

"One girl married some preacher and they went off to a church in Billings. Other girl manages some Chicago marketing outfit. They didn't want the ranch. Not sure they wanted me neither. I moved around doing what I always done. Ranchers sold out, feedlots came in, and the big spreads got fenced. What was left disappeared behind the oil rigs. I ended up here. Chief don't have much ride left. Neither does the mare. Time's kinda winding down for all of us."

Maude nodded in response. They rode back to Harlan's place, unsaddled in a companionable silence and turned the horses out into the little corral. They stood propped on the fence, watched as both animals dropped and rolled, kicking up a minor dust cloud.

"Sometimes of a night I can hear them yipping. Makes me feel content. Them and their wild music. When I die, I'd like one a-them wild critters to be the last thing I see." He turned from the fence without saying anything further. Day sank into an orange-lavender twilight. Street sounds ebbed as neighbors drifted inside their homes for dinner and TV.

Driving back into town, she thought about the old gent. He was comfortable, paid when they spent time together, yet had a respectful reserve.

• • •

A steady stream of tourists and conventioneers poured through Fort Worth as it pushed through the winter rodeo and stock show, toward summer Cowtown Days and the chili cook-offs. Maude stayed busy with her regular clientele, made good money, and enjoyed her independence.

Several times she ran into Harlan at the café, sort of a planned-unplanned thing.

"Fancy meeting you here." Maude smiled her pleasure at seeing him. "No doubt Clem's fresh baked buttermilk pies called you."

"Yes, ma'am. Hollered my name. Besides, thought I might find you here." He opened the door to the café and allowed her to enter.

They sat at a vinyl booth near the kitchen door. Cooking noises, clattering dishes, and shouts of "order up" spewed across them. They sat mostly in silence, had a slab of pie and two refills, the noise substituting for conversation.

One week when they met, he mentioned Chief had died, old age he reckoned. Only the paint was left so they couldn't go riding again.

"My string is running short too," he'd said and pushed his cup of coffee away. "Don't hanker lingering too long."

Growing up with brothers, Maude had learned early how to read the male of the species. She guessed Harlan needed to be around her, although he never said that. Occasionally he talked about his years ranching, his dreams for his son, horses he had known, or the coyotes. She listened, never commented or offered advice. She sipped coffee and respected his private, quiet ways.

Typically, he paid, gave the waitress a tip, and left before Maude. Just as well. She had already broken her number one rule: Stick to business. Never care about a john.

• • •

By late August, Texas temperatures hit three digits and the last of the conventioneers petered out. She ran into an old customer a little after midnight. He and his boisterous group felt no pain as they moved through the saloons.

"Maude. Girl." He stumbled against her. "How are you doing?" An overblown blustering type, he slurred his words.

"Fine as frog hair." She wrapped her arm in his and smiled. "Haven't seen you since last convention. You still working in Amarillo?"

"Yeah. Still teaching. Say, if you're not busy, how 'bout I get rid of these drunks and meet you at the Stockman's?"

"These drunks? You don't look any too straight either."

"Ah, I'm good. Let's catch up on old times."

She cocked her head to one side and laughed. "If you can hold it together, I'll meet you in the Stockman's bar in thirty minutes."

Enrique, behind the desk when she walked in, greeted her.

"I see you still got greasy hair." She enjoyed joking with him and felt ready to gossip.

"Got a new brand of hair oil. Like it?" He laughed and handed her the 216-key across the counter. "Say, do you remember that Harlan *hombre*?"

"Of course. Last time I saw him he was quiet, seemed to have something on his mind. I haven't seen him lately though."

"That's because he got hit by a cattle truck a few days back. Made a mess. Turned over. Good thing truck was running empty. Could have been worse."

Maude blanched, her mood shattered. "What happened?"

"You know that dirt road out past Vickery, off Camp Bowie?"

"Yes, I know the place. He and I rode out and watched coyotes."

"Driver was running late picking up his load. He said he didn't see that old man and his horse. Truck hit them broadside, brakes locked, skidded, then went over." Enrique shook his head.

Maude felt sick. Her heart thumped wildly. "Where is he now?"

"Old man died on the way to the hospital. A deputy had to shoot the horse. Driver got off with a broken arm."

Maude stared at Enrique. "How do you know?" She gripped the counter, her knuckles turned white.

"My wife works for the Tarrant County sheriff. She told me. There was a write-up in the newspaper too." He softened his tone. "Driver said feller just sat there, like he was waiting on something. Never moved, didn't seem scared."

Maude pushed the room key back across the counter. Her hand trembled. "Tell the man that comes looking for me I couldn't wait. I'll catch him next time."

She stumbled toward the door, struggling with her unexpected sense of loss. She walked past several late night tourist shops and rowdy bars with their pseudo good times. The arena corrals, closed at sundown, stood empty.

She walked toward the empty stockyards, unseeing, tears streaming. She tripped on the rough ground, skinned her hand on a post, caught herself and managed not to fall. She felt herself panting, gasping to stay calm.

An eerie, tangible sensation settled around her. Her ears rang. Something trailed her. She felt perplexed, squinted into the dark and struggled to see. Yellow eyes locked on her and advanced. Stopped. Advanced again. She shivered.

Even before the shape moved and materialized, she sensed it. A large coyote ghosted through a thin light pooled near the street gutter and vanished. Silence echoed in the night-shrouded pens. She exhaled slowly and leaned against a wooden gate.

An easy comfort settled on the yards, even the crickets paused. Thankful to be alone, grateful for the dark, she relaxed in the quietness.

"Otie, Otie. You old shape-shifting trickster. Here's to adapting, to changing." She blew a kiss into the darkness.

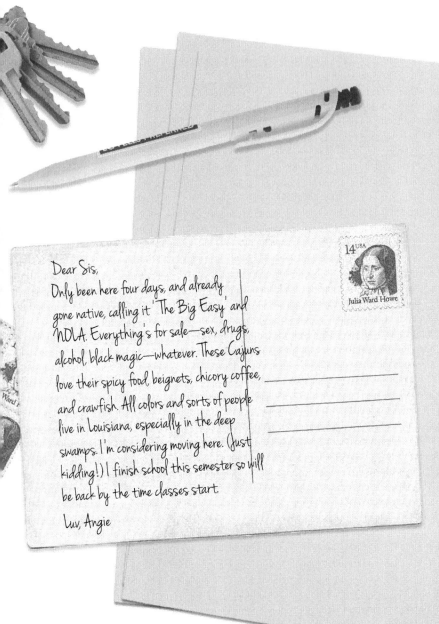

Dear Sis,

Only been here four days, and already gone native, calling it 'The Big Easy' and NOLA. Everything's for sale—sex, drugs, alcohol, black magic—whatever. These Cajuns love their spicy food, beignets, chicory coffee, and crawfish. All colors and sorts of people live in Louisiana, especially in the deep swamps. I'm considering moving here. (Just kidding!) I finish school this semester so will be back by the time classes start.

Luv, Angie

14 USA
Julia Ward Howe

Playing Checkers

Ryan glanced up and watched Felicia Durant strut through the Midtown Bar and Grill door wearing her signature red stiletto heels, hips moving like sawgrass in a changing breeze. An aura of carnality rested on her fine breasts and moved with her like some sunlit storm cloud. As she clicked across the wooden floor every male head in the place swiveled with her progress, eyes locked on those long, long legs.

He smiled to himself, picked up a bar towel, slung it over his shoulder, and ran a sink of soapy water. The night was beginning so fine and promised to stretch seamlessly into the early tomorrow hours.

"You seen my main man Adam? He's supposed to meet me here." Female musk floated delicate around Felicia, black dreads brushed her shoulders and her ankle bells had the charm of rain on a tin roof. The cadence of stilettos underscored her presence and sent goosebumps quivering up and down his arms.

"Felicia, my favorite Creole lady. When are you going to quit that singing gig, dump that white boy, and let me take you to Mexico?"

Still standing, she tapped her candy-red fingernails on the polished bar and blew him an air kiss. "You my personal Yankee favorite who's got more red hair and freckles than money. Driving to Mexico and drinking tequila with you sounds right fine. Yes sir, mighty appealing."

He smiled at the purring quality of her voice and leaned forward on the bar. "Come with me."

"Honey, you my second favorite man. Second." She raised two fingers and winked. "A girl has to go with her heart. Besides, you being what color you are, you burn up in that Mess-eye-can sun."

He chuckled. "We can play checkers. In the shade."

"You play checkers? Like them old men and kids in the park?"

"Yeah, like that. Grandfather taught my little brother and me to play. We had a set from Macy's. Got it one Christmas." He pushed back from the bar.

"I play checkers too. Me and brother had a piece of cardboard we colored off with chalk. Used Nehi soda and Pepsi cola bottle caps for checkers." She threw back her head and laughed aloud. "He move. I move. Jump each other. Whew. Good times in our yard under that big old pecan tree. Just two people. Checkers damn fine game."

He took a deep breath. "Go with me. We'll get checkers and play every day in the park with the old men and children watching."

"You're a jewel. But right now, I'll take my usual and hold your offer on the side for later." She leaned across the bar and stroked his face, lingering for a single heartbeat.

He nodded, turned and picked up a fifth of Smirnoff, poured a double shot over ice, dropped in a twist, and placed it reverently before her.

"You know where Adam is tonight?"

"Don't rightly know."

Twice tonight she had asked about that arrogant, too-rich sonofabitch. He shook his head and shrugged, telling himself to stick to the bartender's code: never divulge information about one customer to another. And, if it could be helped, not even to the cops.

He wiped his hand once across his ginger stubble in a tired, slow gesture. "You check Angelino's place? He sometimes hangs there for a few rounds."

"He ain't there. I've already been by."

She cocked her hip and took in the room with a slow 180-degree turn.

"He likes to have fresh oysters to start an evening. Says it helps his manhood. Nothing wrong with his manhood as it is." She swiveled back toward Ryan, smiled wickedly, and ran a moist tongue across her lips.

"That might be the very thing that gets him into trouble." Eyes low, Ryan concentrated on his washing. His heart always got tangled in cobwebs around her. *Damn. Is a half-truth the same as a lie? How can she not see through that man's veneer?*

She cocked an eyebrow at him and tossed back the vodka. "I can't wait around. Need to get to work. Right now, I'll take an order of cole slaw and fried catfish. To go." She propped her elbows against the bar and watched the room.

Ryan turned to the grill pass-through and tapped the bell. "Hey, Hash, my man. Chopped cabbage and whiskers on the lam."

The sharp hiss of hot oil floated out of the kitchen. Hash nodded okay and hummed a wordless tune while he cooked, his ruddy face shining with sweat.

Ryan pulled drafts for two construction workers at the far end, and busied himself with the waitress-delivered orders. The clientele began its subtle shift from late afternoon barflies and one-on-the-way-home workers to couples too long together, still trying to feel alive, and prowling yuppies looking for a pick-up. Evenings at Midtown began with stale smells, an indistinguishable whirr of words, and the crack of cue on pool ball.

Ryan had considered slinging drinks at the Savannah Belle to be near Felicia. The place had a classy piano bar, dignified clientele, and well-heeled tourist traffic. The Belle's weekend chanteuse, she had encouraged him, said she'd help by opening doors. In the end, he decided it placed him a bit too close to her drama.

On the other hand, Midtown touted a smoky otherworld of fried food, singles on the make, and patrons who relished a hearty belch. He stayed.

At closing, Ryan pulled two short Coors for himself and Hash. Pensive, he sipped and watched as the ash grew on his Winston.

"Five dollars says you can't let the stick burn down in one piece." Hash placed a crisp Lincoln on the bar.

"I got your five covered." Ryan tapped the bill with his forefinger. "You know, a chocolate woman with dreads always been my weakness. Especially one with hazel eyes. Creates an itch down below."

Hash hooted. "You got it bad. Best watch that your head don't sprout another hole."

"Don't get me wrong. They had some fine women in Bricktown. But those women have sharp edges, not like down here. Here women are like cayenne peppers coated with cane syrup. Sweet, with the hot to keep it interesting." Ryan grinned at his comparison.

Hash nodded, untied his apron, and flopped it across the bar. "You know Felicia Durant an item with Adam Reynolds. Adam nothing but a cocky hairball. Him you can handle, but you gotta be careful and watch out for his daddy. That old devil a federal judge over in Fulton County. He mean to deal with 'specially when it comes to his son. He always turns a blind eye to that boy's mischief." Hash stroked his mustache, fingers curving up on the waxed handles. "You better use jock cream for that itch. It's safer."

Ryan raised an eyebrow. "I'll keep that in mind."

The cigarette ash grew longer, bent slightly downward. They eyed the fragile arc.

"Find yourself a nice honky gal that twitches her tail feathers somewhere between sinful and respectable," said Hash. He popped his fingers, swayed his hips and moved to a tune he carried in his head.

"Yeah. You're right. But that Creole beauty got her hands around my jewels like I never had before."

"Better pry that grip loose. Word on the street's got it Adam diddling Mae Pearl every chance he gets. Some women fools for bad boys. Those kind always dangerous. Let her go."

"Can't. I'd do most anything for her."

The ash collapsed. Both men stared down as if they could divine the future in the delicate grey line. Ryan took a last drag on the cigarette stub, sighed, dug in his jeans, and placed a crumpled fin on the bar.

Hash grinned. "Either she come to you on her own without him and call you number one, or she don't. Let the action run its own course." He stuffed the money in his pocket, swilled the last of his beer, belched, and clocked out.

Ryan nursed his brew alone.

• • •

The dream always unreeled the same—she kissed his neck and petted his chest, whispering. "You are my soul mate, my main man, the only one I'll ever love." She moaned and molded her body against his. He arched above her, felt her soft mound against his swollen member, moved against the throb, the ache. Moonlight folded its pale glow across the bed before a cloud drifted past and darkened the room.

Always his dream ended the same—a guttural gasp, body slick with sweat, sheets tangled around him. He'd sit upright, swing off the edge of the bed and grope for his cigarettes.

Hands shaking, he held the unlit smoke in his teeth and waited for the pounding to subside. Finally, he rose, made coffee, and sat alone drinking, waiting on the watery morning light.

• • •

Three months later, fifth night in a row, and Felicia drifted in and asked the same damn question. "Ryan, honey, you seen Adam? Tell me straight."

He finished mixing two margaritas and set the order at the pick-up station before turning to her. He felt his face grow hot. "Give that man up. Come with me to Mexico. We can play checkers."

He waited on the second question, now standard. "Any sign of that trash Mae Pearl?"

"No. Haven't seen anyone tonight." He swallowed but the metallic taste still coated his mouth. He swallowed again and turned back to work.

By the tenth night, Felicia, saucy sway turned into a mean, devil-may-care swing, dropped by. She held her lips in a hard pout.

"You seen Adam?"

Dread draped itself around Ryan's shoulders. He checked every customer seated at the bar for refills and skimmed the room for any potential waitress orders. Finally, he dried his hands on a thin towel, stared at her straight on, and held those hazel eyes a moment too long. He shrugged and glanced toward the men's toilet.

Nodding, she clicked her chipped nails on the bar surface. "Give me some cheap Russian potatoes."

He gave her an eyeball-to-eyeball stare, carefully placed the two fingers of vodka neat, no twist, on a coaster, and slid the shot toward her. "On the house."

Her toe on the stool footrest, red heel hanging down like a dagger, she gazed into the clear liquid.

Several men threw money down and, with exaggerated casualness, ambled out. Streetlight shone through the opened door, then retreated with its closing. A couple of dockworkers picked up beers, moved into the poolroom, and sat on stools, as if waiting a turn. The jukebox record changed to yet another country ode.

Felicia tossed the shot back, turned decisively, and strode into the men's toilet. Pine-Sol and urine odors colored the air. Black and white checkered tiles gave the place an antiseptic look. She flung the stall door wide. It banged against the wall.

Mae Pearl, bent forward, arm muscles rippling and naked tail shining like some virgin moon, braced herself on the back wall. She moaned low while Adam put it to her. Neither changed rhythm.

Deliberate as a striking snake, Felicia hiked her skirt up hip level, pulled a .25 Colt from the garter holster and, without a word, shot Adam in the back. Twice. Powder burns marred his silk shirt. He collapsed forward, groaned, and crawled between the divider and cold porcelain. Mae Pearl let loose with a long screech, her last sound as she entered eternity riding on a single bullet and male cum.

Felicia knelt, tears streaming, twisted Adam's head toward her, and stared deep into his face. "I done told you, I tolerate a lot of things but I can't abide you lying and poking common trash, playing me for the fool."

His mouth opened and closed like a fish out of water. Blood leaked across the cool tiles, viscous and red. Muscles in his neck and shoulders twitched. His right leg shook, his breathing stopped and he lay still.

She squeezed her eyes shut, took a ragged breath, and wiped snot and tears across her face. Gently, she brushed hair out of his face and kissed him on the forehead.

Gun in hand, she sashayed out, paused in the half-light between the bar and the men's toilet, and bared her thigh, tucking the gun away. A peculiar quiet settled. Customers froze in limbo, heads turned. The jukebox clicked, scratched a moment, and Sam Cook proclaimed *The Best Things in Life Are Free*. Three minutes, another record, and Ida Mae Cox crooned long on the blues, trifling men, and wild women.

Ryan stood at the end of the bar holding the edge of the polished surface. He stared down at his knuckles and felt mired in thick mud. *I guess looks can kill.* The song ended, he straightened and tossed the towel under the counter.

"Felicia, honey, I have to call the cops."

He watched her eyes widen, then narrow to a squint. Her forehead wrinkled into a frown. Finally, face held blank, she moved toward him, lips parted.

"Can you wait a few minutes? I need one for the road."

"Yeah, I'll wait."

At the bar, she sipped her vodka and rolled the drink around on her tongue, savoring the mellow taste.

He watched her, memorizing her features, and shook his head. "I wish you had decided on Mexico with me. We could have played checkers."

She placed her empty glass upside down on the bar. "Next time you ask, I'll go. Make the call, honey."

• • •

As towns went, San Miguel Allende was not a bad place to live. Pigeons strutted about, pecking at tidbits only birds notice. The pink façade of the tiny *iglesia* beamed across the park. Mauve bougainvillea spilled down the walls.

He dropped his cigarette in the plaza grit, crushed it with his boot toe, and ambled over to a bench under a jacaranda tree. Two small boys sat in the shade playing checkers, laughing and arguing over the moves. A girl crouched nearby watching.

Elbows propped on his knees, Ryan watched the game until it ended, pulled his hat low over his eyes, settled back, and stretched his legs out.

Memories, things only his heart could hear, whispered in a Cajun accent—*next time you ask, I'll go.*

Second Chance?

The river began an insidious rise, flooding the land, over-taking us even on the roof. Some man in a boat, carrying a pig, sputtered close enough and hollered at us.

"Climb in. Come on, there's room here."

My boy wouldn't go, kept screaming "No! Get the dog."

My wife and daughter huddled together, stared at me, and then climbed into the boat. I slung my boy in behind them. The current heaved against the boat, while the dog, propped against the attic window, howled.

I scrambled back onto the rain slick roof and belly crawled toward the dog. Hanging on to the windowsill, I slammed my fist against the glass, jerked him out through the jagged opening and then slid partway down to the roiling water and the boat holding the mutt next to my chest.

An uprooted oak slammed into the boat stern. Every-one simply disappeared. My boy bobbed to the surface once, grabbed at a rope, missed, and disappeared in that muddy swirl. I yelled, dropped the dog, and plunged into the water, swimming toward the place he went down.

Tree branches, same ones I had stared into whenever I took the children to the park, snagged me in a witch's embrace as that oak floated past. I tried to break free, but I couldn't.

The dog bobbed downriver, whining, paddling hard.

Took the night and most of the next day before a county rescue team arrived. They used a grappling hook to hold the boat steady while getting me loose and hauling me out of the tangled mass. They kept murmuring "easy does it," over and over.

I've been in this emergency shelter three days with wet blankets, cold canned food, and urine odors. And, the acid smell of fear.

Day four, rain finally stopped, and a tangerine spurt of morning light glowed obscene across a partially grey sky.

I used to wonder what it would be like without family obligations. You know, without someone hollering about a lost baseball cap. The bathroom left sloppy. Running late to school. Or piano practice. What it would feel like without a job, your life bleeding out in overtime.

Now, I am alone. No kids. No wife. No dog. No aggravations. I miss the noise, the demands, even the job.

Surprises me, but it's that damn yellow cur I miss most. Not because the dog was special, or my family unremarkable, but because that animal had been a constant reminder of things cast off, things unwanted. Like trash caught in an eddy.

Now, floating in a current of damaged souls, shame's cold fingers dig into my hair and guilt's thick legs straddle my shoulders.

What to do with a saved life, a second chance? Should I hold on or let go?

Dear Sis,

I spent yesterday at Everglades National Park. The rangers tell me there are some panthers here, but all I've seen are alligators, egrets, and turtles. At one point the gators started bellowing—rangers called them mating invitations. Sent chills over me. Water marshes, sawgrass prairie, and mangrove forests keep the area wild. It's different here, rather exotic. Provided you survive the endless clouds of insects, suffocating heat, and humidity.

Luv, Angie

Opie's Fish House: A Love Story

Clayton lit a cigarette and inhaled that first sweet puff, held it, then allowed smoke to coil out through his nose. He leaned on the restaurant deck rail and listened to the night vibrations of the Florida Keys. The buzz of a lone street lamp, the lap of water along the shore, cars crunching in and out of the shell parking lot—familiar, comfort sounds.

Through the screen door, he heard the crash of dishes, Cook grouse at a waitress, and her sharp responding bark. He took a last drag and flicked the butt in a red arc into the bay. Stretching, he ambled back into the glare of the restaurant kitchen.

"Yo. Washy Man, you falling behind. Late crowd swarming already. Get them dishes in the suds." Cook growled, no smile.

Plates decorated with fish bones and butter smears sat balanced on the wash counter. Bowls, encrusted with oil-coated lettuce shreds, were precariously stacked near the drain rack.

"Got it under control. Slinging out plates so clean they squeak." Clayton smiled at his nickname, feeling underdog simpatico with Cook.

Round face slick with sweat, Cook set two dishes on the pass-through and popped the bell. "Pick up." He turned back to the open grill and flipped a searing steak. "Deuce table got sirloin and red fish special with sides."

Clayton respected how Cook ran the kitchen and dared anyone to question his authority. *Good man to have in your corner.*

The pasty-faced floor manager waltzed through and admonished staff in his reedy voice to work faster, harder. Cook scowled, shook his head, and pointed kitchen tongs at the manager's back.

Clayton sprayed plates and pushed two racks into the washer. Steam billowed up. He sweated bullets. Deftly, he rinsed the bowls, cleared the counter, and rehung the spray nozzle in time for a skinny busboy to shove another filled tub before him.

Families and blue-collar workers crowded into Opie's Fish House at lunch while the dinner maelstrom consisted of homegrown high rollers and tourists. The bar, Fish Hook, open until two a.m., catered to a rowdy mixed clientele.

At midnight, Clayton heard a voice he had never expected to hear again.

Unnerved, he slung a nubby towel across his shoulder and stepped toward the kitchen porthole, scanning the restaurant dining room. An elderly couple by the window and five women celebrating a birthday at the round table remained. Already, people at both tables were preparing to leave. He mopped his face, eased around through swinging doors, and turned toward the bar searching for the disembodied sound.

Damn it to hell and back through thick mud. Jack. My brother. Sumbitch should've been dead. He stared at the muscular form at the bar. Thick arms, dark hair, and Neptune trident tattoo.

Frowning, Clayton backed toward the kitchen. He belched, a sour taste rising in his mouth. Seawater smells, harsh brother competition, and spent feelings rippled through his memory.

Again, at 1:30 a.m., Clayton stared through the kitchen porthole. Still at the bar, Jack appeared controlled and arrogant despite his drinking.

Have to give the devil his due. Brother can hold his liquor. Ten years. How the hell did he get here? Why?

"Last call." The bartender signaled closing.

Several customers finished drinks, threw bills on the table, and drifted into the night. Salesmen at a center table ordered a final round. Hangers-on dribbled away in small clusters.

Unable to shake his uncertainty, Clayton focused on final kitchen clean up. He carried the night's refuse to the dumpster, lifted the heavy top, and heaved trash inside. An oily stink, ripened in the heat, rose. He held his breath and dropped the lid; the metal-on-metal clang reverberated through the darkness. Two rats scurried across the plank walkway and disappeared under the wharf. Moths fluttered against the street lamp. Usually, he relished this late drama, but tonight he hurried back inside, troubled.

At two, the manager unplugged the jukebox and turned the overhead lights on bright. A red-haired waitress cleared tables and carried empty glasses, beer cans, and crumpled napkins to the bar, stuffing a few scattered tips into her pocket. Busboy followed, upended chairs, and vacuumed away the evening's accumulation of spilled courage and bottled-and-bonded dreams.

"Want a beer 'fore you start home?" Cook took advantage of a free beer at closing. "We get us a couple from the bar."

"Not tonight, boss, need to get home and let the cat out."

"Always figured you for a dog man."

"Cats got independence, take care themselves." Clayton kept his voice casual. "That tom needs his prowling time, you know?"

"Don't we all." Cook chuckled. "Go on man. I'm jacking with you. We catch you tomorrow."

Clayton's thoughts twisted back to his coastal Carolina home. A lifetime ago, he left college, Canada-bound. Not until '78 and President Carter's amnesty did he meander back across the border to Detroit and thumb down through Ohio, Kentucky, and Tennessee. From Nashville, he hopped a bus into North Carolina.

Six months to travel 1,000 plus miles, working odd jobs and groping homeward. Six days for the final miles to Cape Lookout and the slip where *Fair Weather* berthed.

At each stop, uncertainty gnawed at him, rodent-like. He stayed in the town shadows. Took another week before he could walk the final blocks to the pier and that rusted trawler.

Brown hair tied in a ponytail, he stood on the weathered dock and stared at his dad sitting on an up-ended fish crate. He had sat there the day Clayton left ten years previous. Salt-seared, he glanced up with hard eyes, glared at his son, and turned back to mending nets.

"What's with the hair?" His dad's voice sounded thick, harsh.

"For the cancer victims gone bald. After chemo they lose their hair."

"Yeah? How's that work?"

"Mine gets cut and donated for their wigs."

Dad hawked and spat on the dock planks. The phlegm curled into a tidy wad.

Shore birds scurried up and down leaving white squirts on the rocks. Boats rocked on rope tethers, groaning and creaking with the water's ebb and lap.

"How's Mom?" Clayton struggled to keep his voice casual and face non-committal.

"She cleans the rectory at St. Paul's for them priests. Ought to be home near supper." The old man scowled and bent again to his work.

Clayton shoved his hands into his jeans and shifted uneasy. "Okay I drop by and catch her tonight after dinner?"

"Yeah. You do that. You talk with your mother as long as she'll tolerate. After that, don't come back. Nobody here needs to see you again." The old man turned away, hands fondling the nets with a tenderness usually reserved for a woman.

Clayton simply blinked at the comment, nodded, and walked back down the pier toward town. Only a few hours until she would be home. A gnat of foreboding buzzed in his head.

At dusk outside the weathered house, he lounged in shadow and watched until his mother finished her kitchen chores. He dropped his cigarette into the gutter, listened as it sputtered dead, and crossed the street.

Night seemed to muffle his knock. She opened the door. Light spilled from the living room, haloing her in the entryway.

She stood watching him longer than necessary before she held her arms out. He melted into her stringy embrace, inhaling lavender talcum and raw onion. She appeared smaller than he remembered, somehow sharper.

"I'm glad you come home, son. I've worried." Holding him back from her, she drank in his essence, and gestured him inside.

Thin lace curtains moved slow in the evening breeze. Two pictures—John Kennedy and the Virgin Mary—hung on the wall over the TV. A sagging couch, tired brown lounger, and bentwood rocker crouched around the braided rug, mute witness to stoic lives.

"Old Man's not home. Just you and me." She put a pot of coffee on the stove.

"Where is he?"

"Not sure. He likes to be alone. We both do." She motioned toward the table and a chair. "Sit."

They talked and drank Folgers until moon-fade, his mother succinct with her tale: The family ripped apart by his leaving, their frayed ties unraveling. Jack joined the Marines, running from the small town disgrace of a brother Canada-bound. The Old Man watered his anger and disappointment with gin. She took solace in God, regularly confessed her sins. Love grew moldy, then brittle, finally disappearing in small dust puffs.

In the thin light before dawn, Clayton stood, washed their cups, emptied the coffee grounds, and then leaned against the counter. *Did I ever really leave? Is anything left?*

"Son, you go down to Key Largo in Florida." Colorless and shrunken, she stared at her folded hands. "Not sure exactly where, but find a man named Opie Newton. Has a place called Opie's Fish House. Tell him I sent you." She rearranged the sugar dish and toyed with the salt-and-pepper shakers.

"I'm not sure he's still alive, but he owes me a last favor," she said.

"What favor?" He raised an eyebrow.

"Time was he loved me." She wiped a crumb from the table, allowed it to drop on the floor.

He frowned and shook his head. Clayton searched his memories and unearthed a man that took his meals at their table and slept on a cot in the parish dorm. "Opie? That boat hand? He left years ago."

"Yes." She spoke slow, deliberate. "Not sure if I ever loved him, but he's your father."

"What do you mean, *my father*?" Clayton's voice rose sharp, high-pitched, face contorted into a frown. He jerked his thumb toward a closed door. "Who the hell is the Old Man? He's my father. Isn't he?"

"He's my husband. I don't think he ever loved me. He loved Opie." She twisted her wedding band.

"Loved Opie? What the hell?" Clayton stood rigid, hands clenched, mouth open. "You saying that deck hand—that Opie—is my father? He lit out when I entered school."

She nodded. "Him and the Old Man worked together, closer than men are supposed to. People talked."

"What are you saying?"

"I'm saying they worked together and cared for each other. Deeply. Old Man and I had Jack but that didn't help. People still talked." She wiped her hands on her apron and watched his face change. "Gossips finally drove Opie into my bed. You came along. None of us intended to hurt each other. Things just happened."

"Why tell me now? How am I supposed to feel?" He fumbled with a Marlboro, holding it unlit. Hands shaking, he crumpled the cigarette and tossed it toward the ashtray, scattering tobacco shreds on the table. "Who am I? Some stray dog to be dumped?" His face twisted between bewilderment and hurt.

They sat in silence. Finally, staring at him, she spoke in a steady voice. "We went on another few years, lacerating and punishing each other. Love got to splintering. We each wanted something none of us had to give. Opie left. We stayed to raise you two boys. Seemed the only way."

Clayton sank into a chair. He felt heat spring up behind his eyes.

"Despite everything, that old man *loved you* even after Opie left. I think he put the love and anger he felt toward Opie onto you." She pushed up from the table, pulled out a handkerchief, and blew her nose. "Jack was different, he was Old Man's whelp. Old Man tried to mold him, make him hard, a mirror image of what *he* wanted to be. You were Opie's, so he favored you differently. We all got caught up in too many feelings and worried about what others said and thought."

She stood apart from him. "Things don't always turn out like you expect. Or want." She patted him on the shoulder. "I loved you, maybe still do, but you need go on now. Leave this place behind. Leave me be. Leave everything here."

• • •

Clayton took five days to drift south to the Florida chain and find Opie's Fish House. The restaurant and bar crouched on piles stabbed into Cow Key Channel. Fish and ocean smells permeated the clapboard building. Folks drifted in for the broiled grouper, swordfish steaks, key lime pie, and margaritas. He rented a room within walking distance and settled down. He watched the restaurant.

Days later, he went in, sat at the bar, ordered a Budweiser, and fell into rambling male banter with the barman.

"Well, Opie died about eighteen months ago." Barman wiped his hands on a stained towel. "Left the place to his so-called cousin. She moved to Chicago soon after he died. Hired a management company but retained ownership." He set a fresh coaster under Clayton's beer.

"Got restaurant reviews and tourist chatter about Caribbean ambiance, Bogart-and-Bacall style, and conch architecture. She still calls it Opie's. You know, out of respect." He shrugged. "Whatever."

Elbows propped on the bar, Clayton sucked on the Bud, listened, and responded in monosyllables.

"You looking for a job, check with Cook." The man lifted his chin toward the back. "You make him happy, you're in."

A day later Clayton began his dishwashing career.

•••

Months had drifted by before Jack's voice growled out of the bar and slammed into Clayton's consciousness. Tonight, he finished his work, clocked out, and meandered to the front parking lot.

Jack leaned against a dented pickup in half shadows, hands cupped around his cigarette. He took a slow drag. The tip glowed bright.

Clayton stopped under the neon Opie's sign, dug around in his pocket, and thumped out a Marlboro. Jack tossed him a lighter. Two quick puffs and then a long, deep drag. They stood silent, like two old friends, and smoked.

"Just so you know, Old Man's dead." Jack spoke in a flat tone, no emotion edging the message. "Heart attack. Out on the boat. Some slant-eyed gooks towed the trawler in."

"That why you here?"

"Yeah. Mother said to let you know."

"What happened to the *Fair Weather*?"

"She deeded it to the church."

"Where's she?"

"Don't know. She left, didn't say where."

"So you're here, to deliver the message?

"I thought my beloved, only brother might like to know about his sweet family. The brother too good to fight for his country. You know, the yellow coward."

"Who the hell you think you are? Jesus H. Christ passing judgment?" Clayton pressed his lips into a thin grimace.

"You fucking walk-on-water, above-the-rules saint." Anger twisted Jack's face. "Never could figure out why the old man treated you different."

Silent, Clayton flipped his cigarette into a pothole and stared at the dying butt. "Not the way I saw it. Old Man favored you. He ignored me like common boat trash."

Jack looked away, then spoke quietly. "Had the same mother. Old Man taught you—us—how to handle the boat. How to survive in the water."

"Didn't make me love him. Or you." Clayton clenched his jaw. "Tried college to get away. From all of you."

"Yeah, college was a nice touch until you ran." Jack took a last drag and flicked his spent butt toward Clayton. It bounced off his chest. "God damn you both to hell."

"Not my doing, big brother. Mother tried. Old Man chose you to be his carbon copy. We all choose." Hands wide, he shook his head. "That war was rotten at the core, but I used it. I needed a way out."

"You sumbitch. Day after you run, the Old Man shriveled, shamed. I joined his precious Marines and shipped to save face."

"I had to leave. Turned out though, I couldn't *really* leave. Couldn't start over. We were too knotted together. Nothing worked."

"Sumbitch coward. No one gets a do-over. You take the hand dealt and play it."

"What do you want from me?"

"I was leftover warm spit." He pointed, fingers coiled in a pistol grip, and mimicked a shot. "I'll help you leave, brother dearest. Forever."

Clayton hit him. Hard, in the face. Nose cartilage gave under his fist and Jack's head snapped backward. Reeling, he spun sideways and spat, then wiped a gnarled hand across his cheek, smearing blood and mucus.

Crouching slightly, Jack rammed his shoulder into Clayton's middle and doubled him over. He stood splay-legged next to the prone form and panted.

Rocking up, Clayton balanced on his hands and knees. He shook his head, splattering strings of red slobber. Jack kicked him in the gut, lifting him in the air. Both men grunted with the effort.

Bent, hands on his knees, Jack swayed, his voice coming from a dark vacant place. "Another day, brother dearest. Soon." He spat red and staggered away.

Days later, Jack stepped into The Fish Hook. He placed a crossed-rifle badge on the polished wood and slid it across the polished surface.

"What's this?" Barman turned it over in his hand. "Sharpshooter? Sorry, dude, can't trade drinks for service medals. Offer you one on the house?"

"Give it to your dishwasher." Jack gestured toward the back. "Tell him, Bright Conch Key Bridge turnout. Tonight. He'll understand." He swung off the stool and left without a backward glance, a beer sweating untouched on the bar.

At three, clean up finished, Clayton clocked out. "Cook, drop by my place, look after my cat. I got business." Already his gut twisted and hands shook.

Cook cocked his head.

"Come morning, I ain't back, take him home with you."

"Sure man. Sounds serious."

"Yeah."

Outside, Clayton checked the clip, shoved the pistol into a vest pocket, and thumbed a ride to the bridge.

A rusted Chevy pickup sat on the pulverized coquina shell lot. The pullout marked the last of solid land before the mix of mangrove and water. A few tufts of cord grass, anchored along the tree line, swayed slightly. The cackles of night herons drifted over the water. A wet breeze rose from the ocean, brine rode on its mist.

He scanned the cove. *You deserve credit, big brother. Choosing a moon-dark night.* The sound of a rifle bullet chambered clicked toward him in two beats. Clayton took a deep breath and flipped off the pistol's safety. He waded toward the bridge and slipped into the shadows until he stood thigh-deep in the brine. Barnacles and seaweed slime coated the wooden piers. He shivered at the mucus feel.

A shot pinged off the piling, throwing splinters onto the water. Clayton crouched, his heart pounded. He jerked at the sound of his brother's voice growling, circling nebulous as mist.

"You did bring a gun, didn't you little brother? Don't worry if you didn't. Here's dear old Daddy's .22. You remember it? The one he used and taught you how to shoot?" A mirthless laugh spun across the water. "Tell you what—I'll leave it here on the truck, on the hood. Come get it when you're ready." A metal-on-metal clunk hung in the stillness. "Remember what the Old Man taught us? You know, stuff to keep you alive?"

A breeze materialized. In the distance, the throaty song of Harley Davidson motorcycles floated across the water. Somewhere, a car braked and crunched down a side road.

Clayton squatted partially submerged in the cold water. How had it come to this? This warped mixture. Running to Toronto. Jack sinking into Nam. Family disintegrating. Death harvesting souls.

Concentric circles signaled Jack's slow wade toward Clayton. "You got time to slide on out and hide. You're good at that, little brother. Running's your best talent. I'm coming for you." His voice slipped around the swamp edges, oil on water.

Shaking, Clayton slid deeper into the liquid, glided out from under the pier, and moved toward a mangrove line. He felt his way along, paused and listened for small sounds. A hundred yards in, he stumbled on a root mass, fumbled, struggled to keep his balance as he lost his grip and the gun sank into the quagmire. He squatted and groped blind in the muck. *Nothing. Damn it. I'm naked. Nothing solid between me and Jack.*

He surfaced, sputtered, and steadied himself against a root tangle. Clayton flinched at his brother's whispered voice—too close.

"Come on, little brother. Let's finish this."

A wave of dread washed across him. He swallowed and struggled to avoid gagging.

Carefully, Clayton slid down the trunk until his chin dipped slightly in the water, eyes searching for movement, sound, a shadow, anything. Breath held for long seconds, he listened. Nothing except the incessant buzzing of mosquitoes.

Jack's hands locked around his legs and violently jerked Clayton under. Terror shattered him as his body sank, twining against Jack. Submerged, he twisted until breath ran out and, gasping, clawed to the surface. *Jack means to kill me in this stinking, putrid bay.*

Their watery dance repeated again, twice, thrice until Clayton wrenched loose and struggled toward shallow water. Jack, grabbed his shirt collar, and jerked him sharply backwards. Floundering, they lost balance and fell into accumulated muck together.

Clayton curled over and locked his hands around Jack's neck, feeling the tracheal cartilage. Slow, inch by inch, he shoved his older brother beneath the surface, and held him. Brushing his lips against Jack's submerged forehead, he took a deep breath and lay in a morbid lover's embrace, weight forcing them into a shared grave. Air bubbles escaped his nostrils and tickled up.

The knife slide under his skin and along a rib bone. Clayton stared into his brother's face, felt his hand on the knife, and shuddered. Together, they rose coughing, retching water, desperate.

Jack, coughing and hoarse, spoke low. "You forget? Old Man always said carry something for cutting free." He pressed his cheek against his brother's shoulder, held the knife steady, and panted for air.

"Free." Clayton made a sound somewhere between a sob and a croak. "The Old Man. It's all wrong. If only you had died in Nam."

"Didn't work out that way."

They crumpled against the mangrove tree. With a slow, tender motion, Jack eased the knife out and replaced it in its sheath. A cloud of blood blossomed.

"There, there," he cooed pressing his hand against the wound. "Relax. It's not deep nor fatal." He kissed the top of his brother's head, petted, stroked, and murmured. "My little brother. Hated. Treasured. Shamed. Lost."

Cradled by the roots, they rocked and held each other until cold and exhaustion set in. Jack took a deep breath, bent below the water, and pulled Clayton across his back, gripped an arm and leg against his chest. He struggled upright and waded toward a snip of land, carrying his family burden.

In the east, a thin milky light played across the sky. Jack sank to his knees and flopped his brother onto the rough shell beach. Staggering upright, he stumbled to the pickup and returned with a pack of Camels and his Zippo. He squatted before Clayton, lit two cigarettes, handed one across, and rocked back on his haunches. He clicked the lighter closed.

"Imagine." Clayton croaked his voice unnatural and rasping. "I claim conscientious objection and run for Canada. You go to Nam for the Old Man. Neither of us could really leave. Now, brothers trying to kill each other. How ironic is that?"

"I killed more slant eyes than you've ever seen." Jack spoke quietly. "You want to know what I remember? A water buffalo. I shot it for no reason. Thing kept bellowing and thrashing. A gook woman ran over, crying and yelling."

He held the cigarette between his teeth. Smoke coiled up in transparent spirals. He stared across the cove then leaned forward, his face inches from Clayton.

"Wasted her and put another round in that damn cow." He flipped the cigarette away. "I've killed enough. Time to stop."

He pulled a set of keys from his pocket and laid the rifle on the ground between them.

"Use that as a crutch. You work at it, you can make it back to the pedestrian bridge. Get help from there. You'll be okay." He patted his brother's shoulder, allowing his hand to rest there a moment.

Clayton nodded. "Yeah. No more. Enough death." He curled his fingers around the calloused hand resting on his shoulder. "We'll be okay."

Finally, Jack nodded, stood, and crunched back to the pickup. He slid inside. The engine hesitated, sputtered to life, and dieseled into the dark.

Clayton lay on the shells and broken limestone, blood weeping slow through his fingers. Relief settled around him. He stared at the cigarette his brother had given him. The smoke danced up in spirals and disappeared, a final connection between them somewhere in the ether.

Tangerine streaks filtered across the sky. The bridge seemed a world away.

Acknowledgements

I thank the entire Pen-L Publishing team. They have shaped and improved this collection with their editing skills, book design, and collective creativity, as indeed, they did with my previous book, *Washed in the Water: Tales from the South.* Owner and Editor Duke Pennell once commented 'the job of small indie publishers is to bring along good writers until they are discovered by a larger publisher and the public in general.' Their attitude, commitment, and willingness to publish a second collection has been a priceless encouragement.

I am indebted to Susan Raymond (again) for her original sketches, questions, and comments on my tales. I count her artist and friend.

Appreciation to my writerly companions from the Writers' Guild of Arkansas, Ozarks Mountain Guild, and the Dickson Street Writers for their encouragement, suggestions and critiques. I am privileged to live in a community of talented wordsmiths whom I also count as friends.

A special word of recognition goes to my colleagues at the Fayetteville Public Library for those desk shift changes and weekend trades that have given me opportunity to hone my craft. Thank you to the library management for their commitment to public literacy through their author series, book clubs, and writing workshops—all free.

I am grateful to a cadre of people who offered individual support: mystery author Susan Holmes, Lisa Sharp of Nightbird Books, Norma Brillon, Patti Williams. Legions of others, too many to name here, have honored me by reading my books and commenting. You are indeed valued parts of my life.

In addition, I continue to treasure my own sweet man, Robert J. "Bob" Hartney. He gives me space to create, tolerates my molehills as they morph into mountains, and feeds the cats while I attend conferences and workshops.

About the Author

Washed in the Water: Tales from the South, Nancy Hartney's debut short story collection, won Best Book of 2014 and President's Award from the Ozark Writers League, Missouri. Her follow-up collection, *If the Creek Don't Rise: Tales from the South*, offers another window on ordinary people trying to survive when grit—and sometimes love—is all they have. Her work has appeared in *The Big Muddy: A Journal of the Mississippi River Valley, Seven Hills Review, Voices, Echoes of the Ozarks, Cactus Country, Best of Frontier Tales*, and *Rough Country*. She contributes non-fiction to *Ozark Mountaineer, Do South*, and various regional magazines. *The Chronicle of the Horse, Horsemen's Roundup*, and other horse and sports publications have also published her articles. Southerner by birth and upbringing, she still considers sweet tea her beverage of choice for long summer days. Bourbon and branch take over in the evenings.

FIND NANCY AT:

www.NancyHartney.com

Like Nancy on Facebook: NancyHartney

Special Bonus

Don't miss Nancy Hartney's award-winning first collection of powerful, moving short stories, *Washed in the Water*.
Read a FREE story from the book at
www.Pen-L.com/WashedInTheWater.html

Seven vivid short stories that depict

a cast of characters, innocent and evil,

each reaching out for redemption.

". . . compelling . . . gritty"

"Pour yourself a glass of sweet tea and get ready for a journey into the Deep South, where people live close to the land day by day. Nancy Hartney's descriptions are so vivid and compelling that you'll swat at the flies. These are excellent stories that I will re-read more than once. Hartney is for sure the voice of the south."
~ Ronda Del Boccio, *Write On Purpose*

"Hartney brings to mind both Caldwell and Allison, but her voice at last is her own. 'Last Love' is both gritty and warm, and 'The Fig Trees' is deftly nuanced."
~ Robert Cochran, Center for Arkansas and Regional Studies, University of Arkansas

"This brief collection of stories deals with such diverse experiences as a river baptism and coon hunting while it embraces emotions of love, jealousy, and altruism. The seven southern tales contain some real gems."

~ PAT CARR, author of *One Page at a Time and The Radiance of Fossils*

"No better voice of the south can be found than Nancy Hartney, with her touching stories of life looked at in a most extraordinary way. Hartney writes about people we can love or despise, but most of all sympathize with and enjoy."

~ WILLA Award-winning author VELDA BROTHERTON

"Nancy Hartney's debut collection *Washed in the Water: Tales from the South* is, with the exception of one story, "a gathering of women" that meanders like a slow, drunk river through the landscapes and religious and racial themes of the Old South. From lecherous preachers to lynchings to murderous backwoods boot-leggers, Hartney chews on the violence and beauty inherent in communities from Georgia to Texas."

~ Read the rest of this review by C. A. LaRue at *Deep South Magazine*

"Washed in the Water is an insightful collection, and a delight to read. Hartney naturally, and precisely, captures the hardscrabble Southern voice, which made the characters, surroundings and culture so genuine, so authentic. Her descriptive style flows with the ease of honey over warm toast, painting mind images of place and personalities, while bringing life to the people struggling with their obstacles.

~ DAVID PINCUS

AVAILABLE AT PEN-L.COM/WASHEDINTHEWATER.HTML, ONLINE RETAILERS, AND YOUR FAVORITE BOOKSELLER.

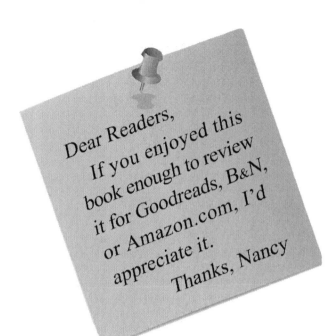

Dear Readers,
If you enjoyed this
book enough to review
it for Goodreads, B&N,
or Amazon.com, I'd
appreciate it.
Thanks, Nancy

Find more great reads at
Pen-L.com

Made in the USA
Monee, IL
13 November 2019

16729826R00122